MW00941968

Good Morning Corfu

Living Abroad
Against All Odds

DAVID A. ROSS

Published by Open Books 2009

Copyright © 2009 David A. Ross

All rights reserved. No part of this book may be reproduced,
scanned, or distributed in any printed or electronic form without
permission except in the case of brief quotations embodied in
critical articles and reviews.

Cover image "City of Corfu" Copyright © Joanna Rosa
To learn more about the artist, visit
http://cyjanekpotasu.deviantart.com

ISBN: 1478375612
ISBN-13: 978-1478375616

CONTENTS

Good Morning Corfu

FORWARD
A LOOK BACK IN TIME

In 1994, I was living in Tucson, Arizona USA and was seriously contemplating leaving America to live in Greece. Eventually, I made the difficult decision to sell my house and belongings and leave my native country, but the decision was not an easy one to make, nor was it ultimately successful. In December of that year, I set out on a journey halfway across America – from Tucson to Chicago – where I boarded a plane on Christmas Day for London, my eventual destination being Corfu. After spending part of the winter in the UK, part in Corfu, and the remainder in Nice, France, I eventually gave up the idea of expatriation and returned to the States, quite dejected. Of course, one failed attempt has not proved telling. After spending several more years in the States, I finally did work up the courage and the resolve to move to Corfu. Recently, I found an old journal that I was keeping which details some of my thoughts and experiences just prior to that first failed attempt to move to Greece, and I found the entries to be not only interesting, but also prophetic.

April 15, 1994 - Tucson, Arizona

Forty-five years ago Henry Miller called America the "Air-conditioned Nightmare". In my opinion, little has changed, except the images are now more sinister. The shallowness, the cultivated distractions, the political corruption – now we are afraid of one another, and there is no trust.

Yesterday in Arizona it became legal to carry a concealed weapon – just as in the days of the Wild West – and I can't help wondering what it might be like to be out in public and looking over my shoulder and into the eyes of each person to try to determine potential danger. Is my neighbor so stressed out that an honest and coherent decision of whether or not to shoot is still within the realm of rational assessment? I don't want a hole in my chest, and I don't want to spend my days wondering about everybody's emotional balance. This life is becoming necessarily insular.

I'm writing my first novel about Greece – I say first because I have an intuition that there will be others. Of course the book is about so much more than souvlaki and sirtaki: it is about these inner battles I engage in; it is about reticence, and about repercussions. The decision to expatriate, once made, seems irrevocable, and there seems to be a huge emotional investment as well. Especially at age forty!

My friend George Delfakis, who lives here in Tucson, tells me that he believes emigration to Greece would be easy – plenty of work for someone with a small stake and a little imagination. Call the Greek consulate in Los Angeles, I tell myself... Just call!!!

December 16, 1994 - Santa Fe, New Mexico

I called...

In fact, I did far more than just call the Greek consulate; I called the Czech consulate and the Swiss consulate as well. I haven't written about this plan to expatriate for eight months, though my mental and emotional deliberations have had many ups and downs: contortions, regrets, reticence, doubts, and spasms... Instead of documenting my emotional acrobatics, I finished the novel: Xenos. And it's splendid! At least I think so. In three days' time I'll be dropping it into the hands of the National Writers Association. Perhaps they will start the publishing process in my absence. That would be wonderful.

I'm on the road in my 1959 Karmann Ghia Coupe, driving from Tucson, via Denver, to Chicago. Two thousand miles of America in mid-winter! The Ghia has no heat. On Christmas Night, I will fly to London.

It's worse now than when I first began this journal back in April – the politics, that is. The Christian Coalition funded the mid-term Congressional elections to the point where the far right now has Clinton on a string like a puppet. He looks scared stiff. He probably should be – I know I am. Many Americans are frustrated and angry, confused, bewildered, but my sense is that it's out of our control now, and everybody seems to know it, at least on some deep level, whether or not they can bring themselves to admit it. This sick drama is wrought with tension married to a sense of powerlessness and futility.

George D. was great! All summer long he fed me scrumptious game from his deep freezer at the Marathon Restaurant. He would phone me around ten-thirty in the evening to invite me for the following evening's dinner, after the restaurant was closed. One night he'd cook venison; the next lake trout; then rabbit stew. All dishes he was not allowed by law to serve his regular customers because he'd hunted and fished the game himself. Night after night he filled me up not only with food, but also with stories of Greek village life (many of which found their way into my novel, *Xenos*) and he also told me about his own expatriation from his home in the Peloponnese to

Canada at age eighteen.

This journey I'm on across America was never meant as a ritualistic farewell. I simply had to conduct business in Denver and store my car with my brother in Chicago. But the trip does seem to be offering one final opportunity for assessment. I'll say it here and now, for the record: I'm hurt by what's happening in my country, by the disenfranchisement of at least two generations; by the hate radio and fear mongering so reminiscent of Hitler's propaganda machine; by the spineless press bought out by the very corporations that control the government from behind the scenes. I harbor no reconsideration about my decision to expatriate. It seems right; it seems like a sound decision. But just whom am I trying to convince? To most, I'm sure I look like an alarmist, a radical. I don't care. To my eye, the Emperor isn't wearing any clothes!

I remember traveling through Yugoslavia in 1989. It seemed then like the entire country had a bellyache. I couldn't really put my finger on it, but it was obvious that something was about to happen. Now, history has told that story in bloody detail. Maybe it's premature to be suggesting some catastrophic civil unrest in America. After all, we've been told over and over again that it can't happen here. We're virtually indoctrinated with the notion that ours is an orderly society. Ah! Wouldn't the status quo love to believe it! But they, themselves, are proving that memory is short, and attention spans shorter yet, and that terrible lessons once learned are not impossible to forget. How self-righteous is this new brand of leader that proclaims not only illegal aliens and Blacks and homosexuals to be the enemy of middle class prosperity and morals, but now academics and intellectuals are targeted as well. Stupid, frightened people are easily led, and easily controlled.

December 17, 1994 - Taos, New Mexico

How easy is it to get hold of your own money in our so-called free society?

My coffeehouse friend Patrick Reilly tried to cash a two hundred and seventy-five thousand dollar cashier's check at Bank of America. No luck. They said they didn't have that much money. So it's become my contention that our money – the money that we think is ours because the bank sends us a statement once each month confirming our balance – this money actually belongs to the Federal Government, or maybe the World Bank; they are simply allowing us to use it, provided we spend it on something they approve. Case in point: Financial institutions must now report all transactions greater than three thousand dollars to the Feds. And just try to assemble a large amount of your own money without leaving an obvious paper trail. It is now illegal to export more than ten thousand dollars out of the USA. We can use the money – our money – as long as we continue to finance the system. It's all too sinister, all too much!

December 18, 1994 - Denver, Colorado

This process of expatriation is not impetuous or impromptu. Many ideas must be examined from every angle and perspective. Comparisons must be analyzed: cultural and political comparisons – even geography. My decision is not a frivolous one. It is not made without due consideration.

December 19, 1994 - Chicago, Illinois

This idea of expatriation goes back several years. I recall talking with Ilse Adler, my German teacher, about leaving Hitler's Germany. I was reading Shurer's *Rise and Fall* at the time and seeing subtle but alarming parallels – or so I thought. Ilse told me about how so many Jews in Germany had read *Mein Kampf* but just couldn't believe it would ever really happen. She told me about how she and her husband were on the last train with Jews aboard allowed to leave Berlin for Palestine, about how the Nazis confiscated her last ten marks and her gold wedding band—but she got out, and never went back. I said to her: "Ilse, what would you do at age seventy-five, with your eyesight failing, if it were to happen again – here in America?" Her reply was straight to the point: "If somebody wants to do you harm, start walking." And she motioned toward the corner of her minimalist apartment where her small rucksack was packed and stored.

Of course I must ask the question: Are my prognostications imagined, or exaggerated, or ill conceived? There are certainly many of my friends who consider my observations to be overly pessimistic. Some have begun to find me tiresome; others have made it known, albeit subtly, that they wish I would just relax and try to fit in. "What if you're right?" they would ask. "What then?"

Ilse must have been in her early twenties, if that old, when she left Berlin. The Nazis murdered her family – she never told me so, but I could see it in her eyes. She couldn't say it, but she knew the end that her mother and father and siblings had met. She never went back to Germany; she never wanted to set foot on German soil again.

I understand that it's now virtually impossible for high school students to find a copy of J.D. Salinger's novel, *Catcher in the Rye*. Apparently the representatives of the Christian Coalition have gained control, or at least significant influence, over many school boards, and they seem to be intensely interested in purging libraries of 'undesirable' literature. I recall being encouraged to read Salinger's tale of alienation and despair when I was fifteen or sixteen. It made a difference in my development, as it did with so, so many others. Of course I identified with Holden Caulfield's cynicism (what adolescent wouldn't?), but the point is that I experienced a sense of identification, and the book fueled my interest in literature. I've considered (mostly a muse) buying one hundred copies of Salinger's classic and handing out free copies a few blocks away from Flowing Wells High School in Tucson. Get your banned books here! Get 'em now! Get 'em before they arrest me, confiscate my trade and burn the blasphemy!

Besides banning *Catcher in the Rye*, Flowing Wells High School, which is now controlled by the Christian Coalition, has censored the students' dramatic presentation of *The Shadow Box* because of its sympathetic approach to homosexuality. Somehow, these administrators have apparently come once again to the opinion that if they can only camouflage the elements of society that they deem unseemly or unfit, then those elements will simply disappear. Or, more likely yet, they can divert public attention away from some sinister agenda they support by creating a pseudo-moral pogrom.

It's not only *Catcher in the Rye* or *The Shadow Box*, it's the systematic discrediting of literature and art that questions the status quo. Certain questions, in and of themselves, have become obscene. Fear has replaced enthusiasm, and so many now seem willing to give up their rights for the sake of some promised order. Of course the order is not real. Nor is the fear. The cultivated ignorance is, however, quite real – it is the legacy of this movement to the right. Hitler employed such tactics, and Savonarola put an end to the Renaissance with a similar movement. To live in a Dark Age where those in control believe that theirs is an enlightened cause! What a legacy! What sick irony!

December 27, 2006 - London, England

I'm simply feeling happy to be away from America. I'm staying at the home of my friends Joel and Chase in St. John's Wood, a block away from Abbey Road Studios and the famous crosswalk where the Beatles were photographed for the cover of their final L.P.

Joel and Chase are themselves expatriates – at least of a sort. Joel works for a big US company in telecommunications. In fact, he's International Director. Big Job! Only I wonder whether he ever considers the ramifications of bringing modern, American-style communications technology to the likes of Poland or India.

These technologies are wonderful indeed – in a technical way. Yet they seem to necessitate a widening in the gap of human-to-human tactile contact. At some point we are certain to be dealing only with symbols of one another, human warmth degraded as a result. I'm not anti-technology per se; still I am more than a binary representation of myself. The subtlest characteristics of personality are not revealed within a dot matrix—the light reflected in a sudden glance, the rhythm of breath or the nervous tapping of a foot.

All in all, Joel and Chase look unsettled here in London. They look timid and uncertain. A bit frustrated and perhaps ready to give up this self-imposed exile and go home to the States. But that's not going to happen, because they've given up control. The corporation is now calling the tune, and Joel is dancing like a madman. Chase is simply trying to keep her balance, all the while wondering what the final price might be. They're fish out of water; it's obvious as their foreign accents.

And what about me? Well, one day after arriving it seems that I'm almost more comfortable than my friends. As usual, my approach to Europe is unhurried. I try to accept this continent on its own terms, so I'll see what the future holds for me here.

January 1, 1995 - London, England

During the past few days a few startling realities have come to light, making the disparity I suspected between American and Euro-economics even more dramatic than I once suspected. For example, the town house in which I am staying rents for about five hundred pounds per week, which is an equivalent of $40,000 dollars US per year. This sum is considerably more than I made working one year in the States. Not to say that some Americans do not make more, but certainly the majority makes considerably less.

This townhouse in the St. John's Wood neighborhood is very comfortable – a parlor, a library, formal dining room, lounge, modern kitchen, four bedrooms, three baths – about the size of an American family-style home – at two and a half times the price!

Around the corner a Pakistani newsagent is advertising for a part-time cashier. He is willing to pay an equivalent of $8.50 per hour, plus insurance and all taxes. A similar job in the States might net the worker $4.25 per hour with no benefits whatsoever. Buying power for the money earned might not be all that different, until the American worker chooses to spend his money out of the States, or on goods made in countries with so-called higher economies – goods like a BMW or a Volvo automobile, or a sailboat, or a South African diamond.

America is presently cultivating 'free trade' relationships with many lesser-developed countries, particularly in Central and South America. This strategy accomplishes several near-term advantages, or so it would seem. First, it provides American manufacturers with a cheap source of labor (good for owners of companies and for shareholders). Secondly, it ensures a steady supply of goods for American consumers (who subsequently fail to notice that prices, as well as their own wages, are falling below the standards of other First World countries, thereby eventually restricting freedom of movement, economic and otherwise, within the world community). This ensures the wealthy business owners a captive work force, or a race of slaves that are largely ignorant of their situation. The working class is codified with an abundance of 'cheap luxuries'. And all is well as long as ignorance is preserved, and there are ample resources to exploit from so-called 'hungry' economies. But, sooner or later, I suspect, the 'cheap' American cost of living will be compromised by a heady round of economic inflation. What then? There will probably be no way to correct a system long out of control, and the long famous and coveted American largesse will be long gone, and probably not recoverable.

September 24, 2006 - Corfu, Greece

That is where my journal ends, quite abruptly. Reading it now, twelve years later, is to me interesting, considering how I've ended up, and not to mention how world events have unfolded, especially in regards to my native country.

To briefly finish the tale that I for some reason did not record at the time, I stayed on in London just a bit longer before flying to Geneva, Switzerland. How cold it was that winter in the Alps! From Switzerland, I traveled into Italy, down the east coast to Brindisi, where I took a ferryboat to Corfu. I remember arriving on Corfu very early in the morning, before the sun was up. I walked from the port to San Rocco Square in Corfu Town and waited for the first bus to take me to Kontokali.

Arriving in Kontokali, I was shocked to see the village in mid-winter. It was nothing like I remembered it when I'd visited during the summer season. Nothing was open, and nobody was about. I found nowhere obvious to stay.

After a couple of hours of searching for a room (word must have gotten round that a winter tourist was in the village), I was approached by a man offering a room at his house. Sight unseen, I accepted the offer, and as it turned out, his wife was the sister of my friend Takis, who was away for the winter in Cyprus. The room that Thalia and Pauli gave me was more or less comfortable, except for the fact that the heat was turned on only for an hour per day at five o'clock. I managed with a few extra blankets.

My original idea had been to buy a small hotel on Corfu – something not too big, perhaps fifteen rooms. (At that time in my life I could easily have afforded such an investment, or so I thought.) For the next few weeks I looked around, talked with people, asked questions; but the more I looked, and talked, and enquired, the more convinced I became that were I to find a hotel and make the investment, I would, in all likelihood, end up broke and with no hotel. I remember feeling like a fool.

At the end of January I left Corfu not knowing where I was really going, or why. Not knowing what lay ahead for me. I drifted over to Sicily and stayed a few weeks at Taormina. Then I made my way up the Italian west coast on my way to Nice, France, where I stayed the rest of the winter to ruminate over my failed attempt to move to Greece before returning to the States.

My restless spirit was not however assuaged. By late spring that year I was in Hawaii; in autumn I was tromping about the Lake District in the UK, chasing the ghosts of the Romantic poets (research, I said then, for a book I never wrote). For the next few years, I traveled back and forth between the States and Europe, always looking, always scheming. Not until 2001, after I'd met my current wife K., did I finally decide to give it another try, this time with all of a thousand pounds in our pockets.

And the rest, as they say, is history!

Much has happened since in the world arena, and also in my native country. Situations I described twelve years ago are no better: in fact, quite the worse. The rich get richer as the poor go scratch. Education is abysmal, and violence is rampant. America has now lost two of its great cities: New Orleans, of course, to Hurricane Katrina, but more specifically to a lack of response from the government in the aftermath of the storm; Detroit is now a wasteland, probably beyond salvage, as the literacy level has plunged below fifty percent. I'm afraid other once great cities are at risk as well. In LA, only twenty-nine percent of young people actually graduate from high school, and I can only wonder what the standards are for those who do graduate. Then, of course, there is the perpetual war being waged in the Middle East (where it will expand to in future is anybody's guess, and probably depends on where there is easy booty to be had). Anybody who has read George Orwell knows the scenario already; *perpetual wars fought in distant lands with nebulous casualties posted on some board somewhere that nobody really reads anymore...*

All in all, I'm happy with my decision to leave America. Of course I miss my homeland sometimes, who wouldn't? But when I really stop to think about what it is I'm missing, I discover quickly that it is the myth I miss, not the reality. And that myth seems to me to be long gone, something I once dreamed when I was but a child, naive and complacent, secure and hopeful. In relocating to Greece, some of those feelings I felt in childhood have returned. It is often observed here that Greece is fifty years behind the rest of the developed world; I say, let it take its time catching up! And do so vigilantly, intelligently! I say to the Greeks: Keep your families together; do not come to value money over civility; respect and value your neighbors – their differences above all! Do not grow fat and sanctimonious, and when your leaders are not responsive, do not be afraid to show them the door.

Greece is in my view a country on the cusp. It is quite literally waking up after a fifteen hundred year nap. The people here are eager and enthusiastic to better their lives, and they seem to see endless possibilities before them. I remember when America was like that, but it also seems a long, long time ago. Perhaps this eagerness and this enthusiasm is the very best thing about living in Greece – that and the longtime tradition of hospitality and civility. I've said on occasion that it was the Greeks who invented Western civilization, as we know it, and they alone have never separated the ideas of civilization and civility. Here it begins with each man and woman, and extends to each man and woman. And if there is any one thing that imparts a feeling of well being, it is the knowledge that one is valued.

Back in 1994, just before I left for Europe, I remember talking with my brother about my passion to leave America and make a new life for myself in Greece. He thought I was crazy. "The fix is in," he said to me. "The fix has been in for a long time, and everybody knows it. The choice is simple: either you shut your mouth and play along with the game, or you move to someplace where the plumbing doesn't work so well."

As anyone who has ever been to Greece knows, we often have unannounced water cuts, and we still have to put our toilet paper in bins, as the pipes here are too narrow to accommodate that particular waste. In short, the plumbing doesn't always work so well. I've now learned to live with that inconvenience; and given the choice between a society obsessed with greed and avarice, one willing to sacrifice substantial values for phony morality, one willing to favor trite facsimiles over insightful art, one willing to cultivate ignorance over enlightenment, one so willing to cast each individual into an insular prison, I'll take the bad plumbing, thank you very much! Yes, I've come home to a place more in tune with the person I am, and the person I want to become. And it feels good indeed to once again be able to breathe.

FANTASY ISLAND

With its long and varied history, Corfu has played host to many foreigners over the years – Italians (Venetians), French and British. These days, over a million travelers per year visit the island, and estimates of ex-pats living here range from fifteen thousand souls on the low side to my own estimate of as many as thirty thousand. What makes Corfu such a compelling place to visit? And what is it about the place that motivates many of those visitors to pull up stakes in their home country and cast their lot on Corfiot soil?

No doubt, the reasons are probably as unique as each transplant. Still, I think there must be a common thread.

I first visited Greece in 1989, Corfu in 1992. As a habitual traveler to Europe (at age thirty-four I began spending every summer away from my home country and traveling for eight to twelve weeks throughout Europe), I came to Greece the first time in an ad hoc way; namely, at the insistence of a traveling companion. I not only fell in love with the sun and the sea, not to mention the cheap prices, but also with the culture. And I still maintain that the hospitality one encounters in Greece is like none other. Back then I often said that even if Greece were not so beautiful, or if it someday became an expensive place to visit, I would come back again and again – for the people! After all, where else, upon his return (even after years) is one treated like a long lost cousin, or a returning prodigal?

In 1995, I dared Corfu in winter. After a couple of visits here, and after consulting with a Greek friend who'd recently bought a fair-sized hotel on the Island of Paros for sixty-nine thousand American dollars, I had it in my mind to try to buy a similar hostelry here on Corfu. Arriving by ship at 6:00 o'clock in the morning in mid-January was, I readily remember, quite a shocking experience. Once the sun was up, I took the No. 7 bus to Kontokali, but found the village to be something quite different than I remembered from summertime visits. Searching for a room, I walked into the village of Gouvia, which compounded the initial shock, as every shop was boarded up for winter. I did finally find a place to hang my hat, and remained on Corfu for nearly three weeks, asking questions and becoming more and more confused, not to mention more and more convinced that I did not wish to squander the money I'd saved on a tourist hotel on Corfu. Nevertheless, the island held its charm even in winter. I returned to Corfu a number of times in succeeding years before finally deciding to move here in Summer 2001.

Corfu is an easy place to make friends. Anybody who's come here has experienced the acceptance that one receives, try or not. The Corfiots are well experienced at having foreigners in their midst, and the other ex-pats, for the most part, are happy to see a new face. I, too, experienced this acceptance here, so it was easy to feel at home so far away from one's homeland.

Yet, any integration into a new (and very foreign) culture happens by degrees, and mine was no exception. From my eight-year plus vantage point, I must confess that life on Corfu little resembles my perceptions the day I arrived here with my wife, our cat, and a laptop under my arm. The old saying, "Wherever you may find yourself, there you are!" certainly applies. Fact is that what and who you are is maintained (with small but appropriate revisions) no matter where you choose to live, and that's not wholly negative. These days, for me, Corfu is simply my home, with all its quirks and imperfections. Of course I still see its innate beauty, but I must confess that trips to the beach these days are infrequent, the restaurants are a bit repetitive, and the surprises far fewer than they once were.

As I see more and more ex-pats coming to the island to stay, I've often asked myself just what is it, on a personal level, that makes one brave such a move. Knowing well that the reality of living here is inevitably different than the fantasy that brought us here in the first place, I can only conclude that it is some deeper quality that makes one long for island life. Perhaps the inner self must inevitably express itself as the outer reality: Are we each an island unto ourselves, and are some of us compelled to act out that solitary mentality in physical, or symbolic, terms?

For me, the transformation to Greek island life, and from first world competition to a somewhat less hurried lifestyle, has been a success. Not to say that I have not seen many during my five years here who have been unable to make the transition. Still, I can't help feeling that the so-called "island mentality" existed within me long before I came to Corfu — to act out my fantasy. Indeed, Corfu (and other like islands) is borne in one's fantasy. The reality, with all its joys and foibles, must prove to be something different, something in and of itself. Of this, I am   convinced.

OASIS

O-a-sis – (from the Greek) a fertile place in the desert, due to the presence of water — Webster's New World Dictionary

During the 1980s and 1990s I traveled quite extensively. In the time spanning 1987 to 2001, I crossed the oceans (Atlantic and Pacific) some thirty times. I visited more than twenty foreign countries, many more than once. While I certainly had a few strange experiences, I never encountered a single circumstance that felt truly threatening. Since 2001, when I first landed on Corfu, I have only once been off the island. So I suppose one can tire of ecstasy, too.

These days, from my sedentary seat here on this tiny oasis in the Med, I can't help thinking that the world has changed a great deal during the last twenty years. As I said, in times past I traveled without reservation to country after country, and without incident, but I fear that the negotiable world has grown smaller during the past fifteen years. Because of politics, or religious strife, or famine, or

17

disease, or what-have-you, I find fewer and fewer places that I might travel to in comfort, confidence and safety.

For example: The Middle East seems intent on courting Armageddon; one hundred people per day (at the time of this writing) die in Iraq by violence; innocent aid workers are slaughtered in Sri Lanka; Islamic Fundamentalism is taking over North Africa, the Philippines, Indonesia; Aids has deprived the entire African continent of two and maybe three generations; violence and starvation ravage Darfor; the Balkans, though mostly peaceful now, are still a bit dicey; only a strong-arm government in Egypt is keeping the lid on a religious/cultural explosion; Britain, France and Germany all have serious immigration problems; and in my home country the literacy level in the city of Detroit has fallen below fifty per cent, less than thirty per cent of all high school students in Los Angeles actually graduate, New Orleans has been left to rot in a stinking, rancid sewer, and one third of all children are medicated (drugged) with Ritalin (or other psychoactive, brain-shrinking drugs) to mainstream their behavior (the ultimate price being the neutralization of creativity!). Meanwhile, we walk through our privileged Western lives under the constant surveillance of video cameras. Is it any wonder that I've not left this little 'oasis' for more than seven years now?

While remote in some respects, Corfu is certainly not cut off from world events. CNN comes piping through my TV clear as the church bell I hear each morning. But like most Westerners, I suppose, the drone of catastrophic events portrayed daily on the news washes over me like an Ionian wave – a big splash that recedes without any real impact. Starvation may be rampant in Africa, and half the world's people may be living on less than two dollars a day, but here on Corfu, this little oasis in the Med, life moves on in a sort of bucolic wonderment. Not to say that we have no problems here, but of course degree is everything, isn't it?

Perhaps I'm locked inside a bubble here. And perhaps the scope of such catastrophic events is lost on me as I bask in sunshine, eat feta, and debate whether or not the euro has been good for Greece. On Corfu, we complain about the decrease in tourism, but let's face it, thirty years ago the cash crop here was olives, not tourists. All in all, Corfu is an oasis, a fertile place in the desert of inequality, strife and intolerance. How very lucky we are in our blindness!

THE FIRST TIME I MET TAKIS

It was 10:30 in the evening, and it was stifling. I felt exhausted and uncertain as I stood with two hundred other people in the sweltering hold of the Espresso Venicia, as the ferry's air-conditioned upper decks were closed off now, and all the passengers bound for Corfu had been sent by the Greek Immigration Officers into this iron Purgatory.

In anticipation of the docking, the porters started car engines, and the noxious exhaust commingled with the all-too-pungent aroma of two thousand live chickens in wooden crates. Given a choice, I might have succumbed to the almost delirious temptation to faint, but my body was pressed so tightly against the bodies of others that there was literally no place to fall.

When the boat finally docked, the mega-ton ramp lowered, and unable to resist the human momentum, I tumbled off the ship and onto the wharf. I gulped the sweet air in desperation and relief. This was Corfu, Greece.

At first glance, nothing seemed obvious. My eyes searched the lighted signs across the road but found nothing that seemed useful. Then I heard a voice. I tried to search out the source of the message but could see only a gray silhouette behind an iron bar fence. What was he saying to me?

"I am a good man, come to my village."

Curiosity was certainly my mission in coming here, but caution was my cultural bias. Nevertheless, I approached the stranger.

Though it was dark outside, I could see his face in the glow of a streetlamp. It was a smooth face, without worry lines. His eyes were playful yet sincere. He was well groomed and neatly dressed. "I come from Kontokali Village," he explained. "Seven kilometers from the port. Everything you need is there--a beautiful beach, a market, everything! I have a private apartment for you. Very nice! You will see for yourself..."

"The ship arrived late due to rough sea," I told him. "I have no Greek money."

"No problem! No problem!" He now spoke with urgency and emphasis. "You need money, I give you money. No problem, my friend!"

What an offer, I thought to myself! So, in a split second, I was obliged to determine if this was indeed a gratis opportunity or a trap. My mother had always warned me as a child not to go with strangers, but of course my mother had never come to Greece. Perhaps the point was moot from the start: it was late and I had no other offers; I was obliged to trust the moment.

Seconds later, we were speeding out of Corfu Town in Takis' beat-up Suzuki. Stray dogs ran in packs across the road in front of the car; motorbikes were as thick as locusts in August. Once away from the port and the superfluity of the city, the night air was balmy and sentient. My eager host spoke in a flurry of imperatives. And even though everything in my midst seemed remarkably strange, I knew that my instinct to come to Greece had not been wrong. I had no idea what might happen next, yet I somehow knew I was in just the right place at the right time.

On our way to Kontokali Village we passed several

open-air restaurants. With music playing, and the catch of the day cooking on glowing coals, it appeared at first glance that the Greeks were inexorably motivated after dark into social interaction. Nobody, it seemed, stayed locked up behind closed doors.

"Maybe you are hungry?" my host asked.

As a matter of fact, I was quite hungry. But of course I still had no money. I nodded to confirm his suspicion.

"Okay," he said. "We will stop at a market and I will buy bread for you. And cheese and wine! You like bread, eh?"

"That's very considerate," I said, "but you don't have to."

"It's okay," he dismissed.

A moment later he veered off the main road onto a dusty driveway in front of a ramshackle building. Instructing me to wait inside the car, he jumped out and ran inside. Amazed by this stranger's energy, and by his benevolence, there seemed little for me to do but surrender myself to his good will.

A moment later he poked his head out of the shop's doorway. Waving a thick loaf of bread over his head, he enquired, "Okay?" I nodded my acceptance, and he went inside again. A moment later, he emerged carrying not one, but two loaves, a one-and-a-half liter water bottle filled with loose wine, a big block of feta, a tin of olive oil, fresh garlic and basil, half a kilo of figs, and ten eggs that he assured me were laid just that morning. "Enough for tonight," he said as he started the engine. I was astonished into silence.

After a short ride, we arrived at Kontokali. Takis' simple apartment proved a welcome reward for my trust. As I waited in the garden, Takis darted about like a nervous mouse, making certain that my quarters were spotlessly clean. By the time he'd finished sweeping entryways and fluffing pillows the hour was approaching midnight, but my host's supply of energy seemed boundless. Apparently it was his practice to smooth over rough edges that did not yet exist.

And it seemed as if he were treating me more like a long-lost cousin than a new tenant. With one arm he lifted both my rucksack and the groceries and led me to my rooms.

Sparing every luxury, the flat consisted of a bedroom, a rudimentary kitchen, and a bathroom. "Okay?" he asked.

Who was I to be choosey at midnight in a strange country? "Okay," I said.

"You are my guest," said Takis. "Anything you need, just tell me. You can stay one night, or you can stay forever. It's up to you!"

"I don't even know how much the room costs," I said a little nervously.

Takis laughed. "Tonight, you make the price," he said.

"I make the price?"

Shrugging, he said, "We will discuss it later. *Kali-nixta*!"

So, that was the first time I met Takis. It was in 1992. Kontokali was much different then than it is today--much more lively with tourists. Takis proved true to his first words to me, which of course were: "I am a good man..." In fact, I still know Takis today. I not only came to Corfu many times as a tourist, each time seeking out the friend I made that night I arrived by ferry with no Greek money, but when I decided to move to Corfu, Takis was there to offer his help. He not only rented me my first house on Corfu, but he also helped me solve many of the problems encountered by a foreigner coming to live on Corfu. Besides being my landlord, he was my friend. Together we grew a vast vegetable garden my first winter here, and during summer we went to various beaches on Sunday afternoons. My first two Christmas dinners here on Corfu were taken at Takis' apartment. Takis introduced me to Corfu from a native's point of view, and we remain friends to this day.

Thank you, Takis. You are my Zorba!

REMEMBERING THAT FIRST YEAR
ON CORFU

My wife K. and I arrived on the 'Emerald Isle' in June of 2001 carrying little more than our clothes, our laptop, our cat (yes, we brought Mr. Felix with us from the States in a carrier that fit underneath the airplane seat), and the hope of a new and better life. My longtime friend Takis met us at the port on a very foggy morning and took us to the apartment he'd promised to rent to us. We got settled that morning as the sun broke through the fog, but I remember little else because we were in a haze from three days of travel across ten time zones.

Once we began to get our bearings, we were pleased with our new digs. Our apartment was cozy, and it was located at the center of the village, just across the road from Kontokali's three hundred-year-old church. We could hear the bells each morning calling the village women to mass. There were several tavernas on the street, as well as a few bars, one of which was just around the corner from our new apartment, and where the patrons carried on till the wee hours of the morning playing loud music. Each night at midnight we could hear the owner screaming

"*Opa!*" as he danced on fire to the music of 'Zorba's Theme.' Did we mind? Hardly. It was all so new and so interesting that we were ready and willing to suspend all our old habits and expectations and welcome whatever came our way.

Later that summer, both K. and I contracted a whopping case of bronchitis. The illness found us just as summer peaked and temperatures reached into the forties. Our little two-room apartment faced southeast, so it took the intensity of the Mediterranean sun, collecting heat all day long, and giving it back during the night. Of course we kept our windows wide open to let out the stifling air, so our neighbors could hear us coughing day and night. It was not long before one of them brought us a kettle full of freshly caught fish and a flask full of that curious clear concoction known as 'Tsipero'. "For the coughing," they told us, neglecting to tell us about the potion's after-affects.

As autumn came, my friend Takis and I traveled round the island collecting chestnuts and other wild foods. Together, we started a winter garden on some land he owned (I did the cultivating as he gave instructions), and we also made plans to harvest the olives from his grove of trees in the mountains. The weather remained warm well into November that year, as K. worked on the novel she was writing, and I became a farmer.

I also remember well an invitation we received from some British friends who lived aboard a boat in Gouvia Marina--an invitation to celebrate the American holiday of Thanksgiving. We really appreciated their thoughtfulness as they served Turkey casserole prepared in the galley of their small sailing yacht. They remain dear friends to this day, and even as it was their first Thanksgiving Day feast, it was not their last. We've celebrated that particular holiday together ever since.

When the winter rains came in December, we encountered our first real problems living on Corfu, the major one being that our roof leaked--not just a trickle here and there that could be remedied by putting a bucket on the floor to catch the drippings, but a full-fledged catastrophe, which left both our kitchen and our bathroom half an inch deep with water each time it rained – which was OFTEN! Of course we contacted Takis, who told us he would see to the problem as soon as the rain stopped, because it was not possible to fix the roof in a downpour. This seemed reasonable enough to us, and we were willing to put up with the inconvenience for a short time, until we came to realize that the rain would not stop until spring, which made for a long and wet winter.

What made the enduring worse was the fact that it was becoming apparent that sales of my latest book were not nearly what we'd expected, and we were seriously short of funds for living. Having very little money even for basics that winter, we harvested vegetables from the winter garden.

One chilly morning in January of that first winter, I left our apartment quite early to do some work at the farm that Takis and I had made (it was located a short distance away from the village), and as I came out of my door and descended the steps to the patio, I encountered a man dressed in a winter parka standing in my garden. He introduced himself as Harry Black, an American, and told me also that he was sent to see me by one of the Canadian women living in our village. He told me that he'd stopped off at Corfu on his way from London to India, and that he needed a place to stay for three weeks. That morning Harry and I went round Kontokali and its environs looking for a room for him, and during the course of our search I learned that he too was a writer, and that he divided his time between the States, various locales throughout Europe, and India. He was on his way to the sub-continent to finish the book he was writing, and he showed me a copy of the manuscript to verify his claim.

During January, K. and I spent three weeks with Harry

Black before he left for India, but the friendship we formed lasted long after his departure, and the next summer our small publishing firm ended up publishing Harry's book.

As spring came to the island that first year, the real glory of Corfu was revealed to us. The weather was sublime, the wildflowers prolific, and anticipation of the coming summer resounded in each and every voice. The people of our village seemed to come out of hibernation as Easter approached, and on the night before the Resurrection, we took part in our village's candlelight procession and fireworks display. On Easter Sunday we were invited to a traditional Easter barbeque, and I was allowed to take my turn turning the roasting lamb on the spit.

And now that the weather had finally cleared, I reminded Takis about the hole in the roof of our flat, and that it needed to be repaired. "Don't worry," he told me. "There's plenty of time for that. The rains won't come again until next winter!" Need I say that the roof was never repaired?

Looking back, I must confess that our integration into not only our village, but into Greek life on whole, was not without peril. But even as we weathered each crisis, there were so many new and interesting people to meet, and novel practices to absorb, that we managed to carry our burdens with not only a smile upon our faces, but with outright glee in our hearts. Such peccadilloes as a leaky roof were hardly enough to dampen our enthusiasm. Our new life was taking shape as that first year came to an end, and we were ready and eager for whatever was to come next. That eagerness has remained to this day, which is without a doubt the very best gift that Corfu has given us. Indeed, what could be better than waking each morning with a sense of wonder in one's heart, and a feeling that yesterday was a good day, that today will be better yet, and that tomorrow – well, the possibilities seem endless as a summer's day on Corfu in mid-June.

PAINTING CHAIRS

Like many people in this enlightened age, my work is mostly mental in nature. I spend many hours each day exchanging information in one form or another, just as many other people do, I presume. Such a vocation may or may not lead to a higher intelligence, but I know one thing for certain: it most certainly leads to an ever-widening derriere.

Since my work is overwhelmingly mental, I experience a bit of brain drain from time to time, so my leisure time is usually spent in some activity requiring little if any mental activity. By nature I am an active person. I find pure idleness to be a crashing bore. I am also by nature a creative individual, and I truly enjoy creating "something out of nothing". I find it highly satisfying to take someone else's cast-off junk and turn it into something of worth and/or beauty.

So, what I do in my spare time (or when I'm feeling just too burned out to write another word, or read a book, or go to the beach, what I do is collect cast-off items out of the trash to refurbish them. Over the past few years, I've found that, here on Corfu, chairs are one of the easiest items to come by. Seldom do I miss an opportunity to snag one out of the dumpster. I store them away until I have some free time, then I set about the task of trying to mend and otherwise reclaim them. I've found that I'm actually fairly good with a paint brush (I can paint a straight line, as well as a circle, which is actually all one really needs to create any number of interesting designs, and I've always had an eye for color), and the result of my effort is a rather unique collection of one-of-a-kind chairs, which are now strewn all about my apartment (at last count there were thirteen of them, and I live in a fifty-square-meter flat).

What I find most interesting about my peculiar hobby, though, is that I seem to have the time here to pursue it. Of course I spend a great deal of time working for my living, but on those rainy winter days, or when I simply can stand no more neural activity, I break out my latest find from the refuse bin, pop open two or three cans of paint (my color collection is vast by now) and have at it. Sometimes I can create the envisioned result in a day, and sometimes it might take a week or more. I don't care. Because I know that when my work gangs up, and I simply must have a break, I can take the time I need. Which is one of the truly great aspects of living in a society where personal time is a right, not a privilege.

It's raining today – the first time in quite a while. I have two willing candidates for renovation in my collection. I've chosen pink and yellow--the colors of Carnival. What do you think? Can you envision the result?

WAITING FOR SPIROS

How many times I have wanted to stand at the center of the 'Liston' in Corfu Town when the cafes are brimming over with people and shout at the top of my lungs, "*Ela, Spiros!*"

No doubt, half the male population in the vicinity would stand up and look in my direction.

Quick to respond, yes, that is the nature of Greeks. And affable to a fault, perhaps. Ask directions and you will likely be led to your destination, even if it is out of the way for the one leading you. They are also equally likely to freely offer their opinions on any number of subjects: politics, sports, the Greek Government (and others, too), food and wine, even their neighbors! There is an old saying that goes, "Twelve Greeks, thirteen opinions!" and at least in my experience, the saying is borne out over and over again. This affability, this willingness to help, this personal touch is perhaps the most appealing characteristic of the Greek culture.

All that I acknowledge freely, but I must also ask (as I've so often wondered), "Why is it so difficult to get a firm commitment to a simple proposition?" Apparently, the simple response, "No, I'm not interested," is perceived as rude, or possibly not satisfactory for some other reason. To me, it seems over and over again that even if a Greek is decidedly not interested in what you are proposing, he will never say so. Instead, he will pretend he is interested, perhaps making a future appointment to discuss the issue, or maybe asking you to call him tomorrow. When you do arrive for the appointment, or make the return call at the arranged time, he is inevitably not there, or unavailable. So you take it in stride thinking, okay, something has come up; I'll try again later. Two days later, he is still not answering your call. Still, you proceed. After all, he said he was interested in your proposal. He did not say, "No, thank you." A week later (maybe longer and after many attempts) you finally reach him by phone, or perhaps you meet him by chance or accident in the street, only to find out he does not remember your name or the original discussion. Why can't Spiros simply say no if he's not interested in the first place? I call this phenomenon, Waiting for Spiros. And I've encountered it time and again.

Of course, everyone who has much experience in Greece knows that 'Greek time' is different than 'clock time'. That fact goes with the territory, I accept it, and I even acknowledge that while frustrating, it is also one of the benefits of living in a laid back culture. Still, it's difficult, if not impossible, to take the bark out of the dog, and coming from a 'let's get it done' culture, I am often frustrated at the so-called art of procrastination which here is status quo. And I'm sure others experience the same sort of frustration, whether they are doing business here, building a house, or some other endeavor requiring timely execution. What to do?

The answer: Absolutely nothing. Sit back and have a cool drink under a leafy tree. Move on. Truth is that it will never change. Truth is that it's pointless to ask why. Our lot is to grin and bear it. And wait for Spiros....

WHEN YES REALLY MEANS NO

When one decides to live within a foreign culture, there are, no doubt, many adjustments he must make, many new things he must learn, and assimilation happens necessarily by degrees. Aside from the obvious differences one must learn to deal with – differences such as food, climate, clothing, and the like, there is a second tier of adjustments one must make concerning things like daily rhythms (what time do people wake up and go to sleep, or what time are meals customarily taken, or what time do shops open and close), how do people pay their bills, or what are the driving irregularities. Of course there is a language barrier in the beginning, and one only surmounts that barrier with persistent study and application. It's not so hard to learn the basics--cordialities, numbers, and even a few idioms. But in any culture there is always a second, far more subtle, language in play: the language of gestures, glances, and verbal oxymoron which is understood only by those who have grown up within the culture, and by those who have vast experience within it. Such so-called nuances take time to learn, not to mention a sharp eye and a few (sometimes catastrophic) mistakes.

For most foreigners, simple existence in Greece is

made both easy and pleasant by the Greek culture. Anyone who has been to Greece even once invariably comments on the hospitality and helpfulness of the people. For a foreigner who comes to Greece to live, this does not change--especially on the exterior. In fact, it may even escalate once they realize that you've chosen to stay permanently in their village, and once you've learned a few words of the Greek language. Every culture seems to respect foreigners who make even the smallest effort at integration. When I first came to Corfu to live, one of my neighbors, on learning that I meant to stay, almost immediately began teaching me the everyday expressions she knew I would need: *Kali-mera; kali-spera, ey-kar-h-sto.* The first year I was here I was even invited to Christmas dinner in the home of a Greek family.

But what about those subtle gestures, and those expressions that, even when you learn the literal meaning of the words being spoken, you are still at a loss to understand?

Without question, this takes more time. Not to mention the will to unravel the puzzle. Still, I must confess that I did not even begin to gain insight into this far more subtle language until I actually began working within the culture. And it did not happen automatically. At first, these nuances became more cryptic, not less so. I was interacting for the first time on a much different layer of the culture, and my mistakes were many, my frustrations sometimes profound (and certainly prolific). For example, what exactly was meant when the person I was talking with turned up his palms and ever so slightly glanced upward?

Here are a few more such examples: It is often noticed by foreigners that young Greek women these days walk around with the most dour of expressions on their faces. In many cases they seem quite unapproachable, as if they might rip your face off, or call a cop, if you even dare to speak to them. Yet, when one does break through the proverbial ice, one often finds the sweetest nature is concealed beneath the sourest facial expressions. One might ask: What do they have to be so glum about? After all, they live a life that we, for the most part, have only dreamed of living.

And who has not encountered the old widow, dressed all in black, who seems, when one passes, to be giving the evil eye? Yet, when greeted in her own language, she breaks into a (sometimes toothless) smile that makes even the Ionian daylight pale by comparison.

When I began actually doing business here on Corfu, I naturally brought with me my own cultural biases of business protocol. It did not take long for me to understand that not only did I sometimes misunderstand what I was told, but that those to whom I was speaking often regarded me quizzically. I quickly got an education-- one that is by no means complete after several years of observation, practice and experience.

Here is one conundrum that, to this day, I fail to always recognize, nor to understand: When offered a proposition, a Greek will never say no directly, he will never dismiss your suggestion out of hand; instead, if he is actually not interested, he may tell you that he is interested, but not right now, maybe later, come back next month. At the beginning of my involvement on this level, I took these people at their word; I took them literally. When I did come back next month, I received a cordial welcome, but I also noticed puzzlement as to why I'd returned with the same or similar proposition that they'd heard a month earlier. One might think at this stage that the person who was not interested in the proposal would dismiss the notion once and for all and simply be done with it. Not so here in Greece. Instead, he will likely tell you he's not quite ready yet, maybe next year. When next year comes and you return, you may well again be welcomed, he may ask how your endeavor is going, but his excuse will be something a bit more creative--never dismissive, always hopeful, even a bit encouraging, yet nevertheless frustrating.

At first I interpreted such put-offs as a product of the *meta avrio* culture. Why do today what one can put off till tomorrow? But it's not that at all. After a fair amount of tail chasing, I've now learned (at least some of the time) to understand that in this culture yes often means no. Still, when to interpret such signals literally, and when to understand that it will do no good to beat a dead horse, often eludes me. Like a silly puppy, I sometimes am caught dancing in circles, chasing the tail I shall never quite catch up with.

I must admit, though, that I'm better at interpreting these subtle signals than I once was, and thankfully so. I spend less time retracing my steps, which I can only imagine must be an embarrassment for those I call on after a (refusal?). Lucky for me, nobody seems to hold my cultural ineptitude against me, and even those with whom communication has broken down on some level usually offer me a drink, as well as their best wishes.

To say the least, doing business in this country has allowed me to penetrate the culture in ways that those who do not participate in everyday commerce might never gain. I'm not complaining; though I'm still sometimes frustrated by my lack of understanding, the experience has taught me to see not only work, but also other everyday rituals in quite a new way. And isn't that what cultural integration is all about?

These days, when talking with a prospective client, and finding that I'm at a loss to understand his reasoning about one topic or another, I find that I often turn up my palms, raise my glance ever so slightly, click my tongue, and lift one eyebrow slightly. I may not know specifically what these gestures mean, but I have nevertheless assimilated them into my own body language, and somehow, it seems, we understand one another just a bit better than we might once have understood

LITTLE ITALY

In New York City there is a neighborhood called "Little Italy". It is the part of the city where many of the Italian immigrants of the nineteenth and early twentieth centuries chose to congregate and make their new homes. The neighborhood endures to this day, its residents still mostly of Italian descent and still speaking their native tongue and observing Old World customs.

New York has other such ethnic boroughs, as do many American cities. In Chicago, where I grew up, there are large neighborhoods consisting of Polish immigrants, German immigrants, Scandinavians, Irish, Italians and yes, even Greeks. Boston is home to a prolific number of Irish immigrants, most of them having arrived in the States destitute, or fleeing from political or religious strife. San Francisco has an extravagant China Town, where the streets resemble those in Shanghai or Hong Kong. More recently, Viet Namese neighborhoods have emerged in many American cities, as well as enclaves of Koreans and other Southeast Asians, and many, many immigrant from the Arab countries in the Middle East now call America their home. The western part of the USA is now home to so many Mexicans and other South Americans that

Spanish language lessons are now required by law in many schools.

These days, Europe – and especially the UK – has issues with immigration. I was recently told that in Manchester alone no less than one hundred twenty-seven languages are spoken. Many British people I've talked with here on Corfu (let's not forget that most of them are new immigrants themselves) bemoan the recent influx of foreigners to their homeland. The major argument seems to be not racist in nature, but cultural, that the immigrants tend to cluster together, taking over urban neighborhoods for themselves, refusing to learn the English language or adapt themselves to English customs. Then, of course, there is the issue of entitlements.

In my home country, nearly everyone is an immigrant of sorts. Even the oldest Caucasian families date back no more than a few generations. The exception being, of course, the Native Americans, whom the newcomers nearly wiped out completely in a thoughtless and brutal act of genocide, which is perhaps equal to none other the world has ever known. These days, in America, intermarriage between ethnic groups is a fact of life--not only in the older, Caucasian groups, but also among ethnic groups who presumably never before mixed their gene pools: Mexican-Irish couplings are common; Caucasian-Asian marriages are passé; and I've encountered such seemingly odd mixes as Peruvian-Czech and Korean-Creole. In the States, Jews have been marrying Catholics for years; Muslims marry Christians; Buddhists marry Atheists. America has been known for years as the "melting pot" of the world, but in reality we are the world's premier hybrid culture, a grand experiment in the mixing of races and cultures.

Of course, the mixture is not always easy. Black people of African descent endured slavery for more than a century, and even after their liberation have experienced racial persecution and inequality--even more so than in

Europe. Mexican gangs wage war with one another over turf in LA, and the Chinese do likewise in San Francisco. The Polish and the Jews are often maligned with racial slurs from ignorant people. Hey, it's far from a perfect world!

Here on Corfu the immigrant situation is at play, too. The only difference is that the immigrants here are largely, though not exclusively, European. The British Consulate here on Corfu has some fifteen thousand British registered as residents, but not every Brit living on Corfu registers with the Consulate, and the reality, I suspect, is more like twenty thousand British ex-pats. There are also several thousand Dutch living here, many, many Germans and Austrians, Scandinavians, Serbs, Australians, Canadians, and yes, even one or two Americans. And then, of course, there are the Albanians – several thousand strong!

It occurs to me that many of the people I speak with who decry Britain's so-called immigration crisis are indeed immigrants themselves. So, who's calling the kettle black, my friends?

Not long ago I did a bit of research on the subject of immigration in my home country, and was not particularly surprised to learn that during the short history of immigration to the USA (we're talking about only a few hundred years) an immigrant typically produces eight times what he consumes during the course of his lifetime. Indeed, if that is the case, then it would do all countries well to fling open the gates to these souls who seek a better life, thereby ushering in an economic boom for which no one would be poorer. Imagine living in a country where economic growth is eight times what it is now, the USA during the nineteenth and twentieth centuries being a case in point! Not to mention the cultural growth we might all participate in if we simply tolerate rather than dictate conformity. Historically, let's remember, that the notion of racial purity has failed miserably when tried, and I, for one, have long entertained the idea that the mixing of races does not corrupt the gene pool; rather, it enhances it. Fresh water always tastes better than that drawn from a stagnant pool.

It is August now, and on Corfu that means, of course, that the Italians have arrived for their holidays. Each year in August Corfu become "Little Italy", as the island is flooded with visitors from Naples, Rome and other Italians cities and towns. They arrive by ship, groups of young boys sleeping six to a room, couples in their cars packed with Italian products, from bottled Italian water to Italian espresso, from *prociutto* to Parmesan cheese. (It seems they can't live without a few of the comforts of home.) Most speak no Greek and little English. They mostly stay to themselves, even as they create mayhem with their motorbikes on the roads. For many people living here, the three or four weeks in August when the Italians come is a test of patience. Nevertheless, and in the traditional Greek way, hospitality is extended, and tolerance is observed. After all, in the ancient Greek culture the practice of *philoxenia* was (and still is) a given. The practice itself comes from a long-standing mythological tradition, one that suggests a foreigner should be treated well, because he just might be a god in disguise.

Perhaps we in Western cultures might do well to take a page from that book.

THE PRIEST, THE BARBER,
AND THE VILLAGE IDIOT

In my village, as I'm sure is true in all villages on Corfu and throughout Greece, the priest is a central character. Of course there is no mistaking him, as he wears a long black robe, a funny hat, and hasn't shaved since Greece was liberated from Turkish rule. He is seen almost daily in the village, whether performing some religious rite or simply greeting villagers.

I am not, of course, Orthodox. Nor am I even Christian. Yet neither of those facts has prevented me from interacting with the village priest from time to time. One New Year's Day I was walking through the village on my way to a hearty roasted lunch, when I was stopped in the street and summarily blessed by the priest. It did not seem to matter to him that I was obviously not Greek, and he never inquired whether or not I was Christian, or whether I wanted to receive the blessing. I, in turn, accepted the gesture graciously and thanked him with a nod.

Likewise, when I moved into the apartment where I now live, the priest was summoned by my landlord to bless the premises before K. and I occupied it. The priest made an incantation (which could have been either a blessing or a curse for all I could determine), and he placed an ashen cross over the threshold of my door, which remains there to this day.

Yet my most prolific, and by far most memorable, encounter (or should I say encounters) with the priest have been vehicular in nature. The village priest drives a car (a fifteen-year-old Volkswagen), but I'm sorry to report that his driving skills are more than a bit wanting. On more than one occasion he has nearly run me down as I passed on my bicycle. I don't think for a moment that these near accidents are purposeful or malicious; rather I'm convinced that the poor old guy just doesn't see very well and is reluctant to wear glasses. Still, these near misses have made an impression on me, and whenever I'm riding my bicycle and see the intrepid VW approaching, I steer clear and give a wide berth.

Another quintessential figure in our village is the barber. If you've ever been to our village, you've probably noticed his shop. It is a tiny walled-in enclave beneath a staircase. When he is ready for business the door to his shop is left wide open, and one can see inside. There is only one chair, and if one chooses to wait as he cuts the hair of another, the chairs are outdoors.

When I first moved to Kontokali, I tried to enlist the services of the village barber, but I was sternly dismissed, turned away. The man simply refused to cut my hair. I was not only a bit put off by the dismissal, but quite puzzled as well. A few days later I tried again, and once again I was refused service. Even more mystified by his behavior, I asked my friend Takis why I'd been refused service. After all, all I wanted was a haircut! Takis was wont to explain the barber's odd behavior, and to this day the man has never cut my hair. I've since found another source for this periodic need, but I still do not know the reason that I'm apparently banned from his little cubicle beneath the staircase.

Then there's Kontokali's version of the village idiot. He is an older man who sits outside one of the cafes each day. His sole purpose in life seems to be to render a vociferous greeting to each passer-by. With an idiotic smile on his face, he hails both Greeks and tourists alike with a salutation and a little song, and I sometimes wonder: What does this senile old man know that the rest of us have yet to learn?

I suppose most Greek villages have their own version of these three characters, which, coming from a culture where such things have never existed, tends to amuse and sometimes even thrill me. Each of these characters is an essential element of the village, and odd or crazy as they might be, nobody would think to minimize their presence. I may not need to be blessed by the village priest, and I may indeed have to find a replacement barber, but when I pass the old man's chair and find that he is not there to shout out his idiotic greeting, I inevitably wonder if he's all right, and if he'll be sitting there next time I pass. Such characters as these seem to me to be a throwback in time, yet each is indeed something of a treasure. Our village would not be the same without them, and everybody here seems to realize their importance. Which, to me, is the really important message in this account.

HOW THEY COME AND GO

Living in Kontokali, I see quite a few transients during the course of the summer. Of course Kontokali, as a tourist destination, is but a shadow of its former profile. Talk with any of the local people about Kontokali's precipitous decline in tourism, and they are likely to remember a time not long past when the streets of the village were thronged with visitors during summer. Sadly, or perhaps not so sadly, those days seem to be gone.

These days, the one attraction remaining for this once popular tourist village is Gouvia Marina. It is by all accounts a first class facility, so many of the itinerants one encounters in the village have moored their boats and are here for either a long or short stay at the marina. As a result, the tourists, or visitors, one typically finds in Kontokali these days are not week-long package holidaymakers, rather they are the more salt-of-the-earth variety, sailors and those somehow involved in the pastime of sailing. They are quite a colorful lot, to say the least, and if one is fortunate enough to get to know some of these visitors during their stay at Gouvia Marina, he is lucky indeed.

One of the first people I met here in Kontokali, other

than the Greeks in my immediate vicinity, was a fellow named Bertie. He was an Irishman who was acting as the skipper of a yacht moored in the marina. Talking with Bertie one afternoon at the Beer Bucket, I learned that he had spent some time living in my home city in the States. We swapped a few stories about Denver while drinking large bottles of Amstel as a toast to each one - or so it seemed. As the summer progressed, I met a few other sailors from the marina (DH, an ex-Special Services war horse; OD Alan, a quiet man from the North country; Scottish Jimmie, whom I failed miserably to understand due to his thick brogue) and I fell in with their afternoon drinking crowd (my own thirst, I must confess, was no match for theirs).

Later that summer, however, Bertie abruptly disappeared. Word went out that he'd left rather suddenly for Spain. His departure seemed to me to be a bit premature, so I asked around about it. Apparently, he'd insulted one of the Greek women in Kontokali by making (in jest it was presumed, but not confirmed) a sexual innuendo about the woman's daughter (who was undeniably very attractive). Whatever old Bertie had meant by his off-color comment, innocent or otherwise, the meaning was apparently lost in translation. I'm not exactly sure why he left so suddenly, but I think I can safely assume that his decision was taken with some amount of encouragement from the local Greek population.

That same year, though in late autumn and early winter, I remember another rather colorful figure here in Kontokali. Otto, a Dutchman of ninety-nine, was staying aboard one of the yachts anchored in the marina with his daughter and son-in-law. Otto's ambulatory prowess had apparently long since deserted him, and he was confined to a wheel chair, though that hardly seemed to stop him from getting round the village. (Whether or not his mental faculties were intact is quite another matter altogether). On any number of occasions, I saw old Otto driving his motorized chair down the streets of the village, traffic backed up behind him, with drivers honking and cursing for him to yield the way. Seeming not to hear the car horns (or the explicatives), Otto continued on his way without pause or concern. (Where he might have been going is anybody's guess). All throughout the winter, he was a familiar (if obstructive) figure on the streets of Kontokali Village.

Another fellow I remember well was Harold; also known as 'Swampy'. He was a young guy who had, according to his own account, inherited a good deal of money. Most would agree, I think, that inheriting money at a young age is somewhat fatal (at least for the fortune), but the supposed largesse was hardly Swampy's claim to fame. What was remarkable about him was the fact that, by his own account, he'd done virtually every type of job known to humankind. He'd worked as a pilot; he'd been a parachutist; he was a master sailor; he'd been a commodities trader, and so on. As Swampy's stories multiplied, it became a standing joke around the village that if he'd indeed done everything he said he'd done, then he would have to be one hundred eighty-seven years old. Still, expressed doubts did not seem to deter him one bit; each week, it seemed, a new and fantastic story passed over his lips (albeit, between sips of his favorite libation).

Swampy became a familiar figure around the marina and in the local pubs. His fabrications were both harmless and amusing. Until the unfortunate circumstance that instigated his rather sudden departure...

Asked by another yachtsman to look after his boat while he was away, Swampy (the master yachtsman) quickly accepted the job. Apparently, all went well for the first week of his employment, but one night during the second week, the yacht he was looking after caught fire, burned, and sank to the bottom of the sea in Gouvia Marina. Quick to deflect responsibility for the sinking of the yacht, Swampy went into action, telling a few outlandish tales about how and why the boat had sunk. Of course nobody gave his excuses much credence, and fearing the wrath of the owner (not to mention financial responsibility for the yacht), Swampy disappeared, like a shadow after dark, from Kontokali Village. A few days later, the Greek police were seen going from boat to boat in the marina asking after the whereabouts of (you guessed it) Mr. Swampy.

Still another habitual itinerant in the village is Dr. Wolfgang Lidl. Certainly past seventy years of age, Dr. Wolfgang, a retired Austrian Army surgeon, turns up from time to time. My friend DH lovingly calls him 'The Old Nazi' (in jest, of course, but to his face), yet DH and Dr. Wolfgang are great friends. Each time I see Dr. Wolfgang walking deliberately down the street with his small suitcase in hand, I know that there will be a raucous party that night at the Navigator's Bar, as DH and 'Wolfie' like to paint our small village four shades of red each time the good doctor visits.

Dr. Wolfgang never stays long in the village (usually only a few days, and a couple of weeks at most), but his visits never fail to lend the scene a little color. Last summer, Dr. Wolfgang was seen parading about the village for the better part of two weeks wearing his grandfather's Austrian Cavalry uniform (and let's not forget, that takes us back a few years). Clad in his dress whites and his cavalryman's cap, Wolfgang cut quite a figure as he sat on the patio at the Navigator's Pub. (I must say that I'm looking forward to Wolfie's next visit, just to see how his taste in fashion might have evolved during his winter stay in Namibia!)

These are just a few of the colorful figures that give Kontokali Village its unique character. There are many more from the past, and there will no doubt be a few new faces come next summer. Thinking about the somber faces of the businessmen dressed in their black and white suits on the tube each morning in London, I can't help feeling that we here in ramshackle Kontokali are rather lucky to know some of these off-beat characters. Long may they visit our humble village!

A WINTER GARDEN

Shortly after moving to Corfu I began writing a novel entitled, *A Winter Garden*. The book was a sequel to a previous novel I'd written in 1994 entitled, *Xenos*. The title of the second book was derived from the real life experience of growing a large winter garden with my friend Takis.

All during the autumn of my first year on Corfu, I tilled soil and prepared plots, all the while assured by Takis that we could grow a bountiful crop of vegetables on Corfu during winter. "The rain will come in November," he told me. "After three months, we will take many vegetables." Having no other gainful employment on Corfu, I approached the work enthusiastically.

My approach to growing a garden, however, was somewhat different than that of my Greek partner. I was inclined to plant seeds along neat rows in well-defined plots. I created furrows to trap the water. I dug out weeds and worked fertilizer into the soil. Takis, on the other hand, scoffed at my approach. "No need for that," he explained as he cast a handful of seeds haphazardly onto the ground. "On Corfu, everything grows," he assured me.

In my carefully laid out rows, I grew carrots and celery,

onions and garlic, spinach and lettuce, as well as a variety of other greens recommended by Takis. My friend, on the other hand, grew a crop of potatoes, as well as a bean plant I'd never seen before called *kukia*. It was the seeds that produced that bean plant that he'd scattered wildly about the land adjacent to my plots, seeds I never really expected to germinate and produce plants.

Takis was also quite enthusiastic about harvesting wild greens. In Greece, such wild plants are used for salads and as cooked vegetables. The Greek word for these wild plants is *xorta*. Takis seemed to know exactly which wild plants were edible, and each day at our winter garden he collected a large bagful of what I came to call Takis' weeds. Back at my apartment, he separated the various plants, cleaned them quite thoroughly, and then boiled them on my cook stove for his lunch. The smell they gave off while cooking was nothing short of rancid, and I only tried his wild vegetable ragout once, which was one time too many.

As the season progressed, the rains came, but not as Takis had hoped. It was a dry autumn on Corfu, and a cold one as well. The seeds we'd planted germinated slowly, and the plants that emerged were stunted from the cold nights. Still, we managed to harvest a few vegetables. The one crop that did well, oddly enough, was the bean that Takis had scattered. The plants grew tall and proud and produced a foot-long bean in abundance. I, too, harvested some of the beans, and when my Greek neighbor Frederiki saw me washing them in my garden, she cautioned me: "The *kukia* bean must be boiled twice before eating it, otherwise it was poison." Feeling a bit skeptical about eating the beans, I told Takis what Frederiki had told me, but he said that that was nonsense, and that he'd been eating them raw his entire life. My skepticism was not assuaged; after all, this was a man who ate weeds for lunch!

In the end, I decided to heed Frederiki's warning, and I did indeed boil the beans twice. They were delicious. Takis, on the other hand, ate them straight out of the garden. (I knew this for a fact, because when I would arrive each morning at the garden to work, I often saw one of the Kukia bushes stripped clean, and I knew that Takis had already been there that morning and taken his breakfast in the raw, so to speak.)

By the time spring finally came, and it was time for tourists to begin arriving on Corfu, Takis had been eating the beans for a couple of months. The garden was left for me to tend, as Takis turned his attention to renting out rooms. Each day I went to work in the garden, while Takis went to the port to meet the incoming ships--an easy and carefree arrangement, except for one small problem. Takis had developed a large boil on his upper lip, which was both painful and unsightly. The cause of the malady remained a mystery, even to Takis' doctor. The boil was lanced and a salve was prescribed, one which turned Takis' lips as purple as an eggplant. Still, Takis was dedicated to the treatment, and each day he arrived with swollen purple lips.

"It's the *kukia* beans," Frederiki told me when she saw Takis' mouth. "You have to boil them twice!" she maintained. I told Takis about Frederiki's diagnosis, but he scoffed once again. "I've been eating those beans raw my entire life," he reiterated.

The problem grew worse by the day. In time his entire mouth became infected and swollen. As a result of the infection, he was unable to shave, which only added to his increasingly grotesque appearance. "I can't go to the port looking like this!" he groaned. "Perhaps you should stop eating the beans," I suggested. Of course he wouldn't hear of it.

As the spring advanced, and the rain ceased, and the winter garden gradually began producing fewer and fewer vegetables. The spinach and the lettuce withered, the roots were finally all harvested, and even the *kukia* bean plants finally failed to produce fruits. It was then, and only then, that Takis' mouth infection began to heal. Once again he was able to approach arriving tourists without embarrassment.

For me, the experience of growing a winter garden on Corfu proved not only novel and enjoyable, but profitable as well. (Money was very tight that winter, and often the vegetables harvested in the winter garden went into the soup that graced our table.) The harvest I claimed was, however, somewhat different than that of my friend. Besides the sustenance taken from the fruits of my labor, the harvest provided me with the literary metaphor that brought the book I was writing to life. Takis, on the other hand, still carries a scar on his upper lip left by the persistent boil.

These days the plot where we grew the one and only winter garden has gone back to weeds. I've not visited the land lately, but I'm sure that Takis still harvests *xorta* there. I, on the other hand, buy my vegetables from the green grocer. No weeds for me, thank you. I prefer to know the consequences of what I put in my mouth before I chew and swallow, because I can't help thinking that what goes in must eventually come out in kind.

A SMALL FORTUNE

Question: How do you make a small fortune on Corfu?
Answer: Arrive with a large one.

My life has certainly had its ups and downs. I've ridden the roller coaster, so to speak, especially concerning the subject of money. There have been times when I've been very well off, and there have been a few times when I've been forced to sleep in my car. Most of us tend to worry about money, which is to say, "Will we have enough of it?" But just how much is enough? Many of us tend to equate having money with having security, but seldom does money prepare us for the so-called broadside accident. Money can sometimes solve certain crises, but it seldom offers redemption in a truly life-changing situation.

Many people say, "If I could only win the lottery..." But research suggests that lottery winners often are far more miserable after their big win than they were before it happened. Still, many of us maintain that we'd take our chances in that regard.

Even before I was forty years old I had acquired a good deal of money, most of it coming in a relatively short period of time. The truth is that, for me, while it did change how I 'spent' my time somewhat (at least for a while), it did not bring me any resounding comfort, nor did I feel any different than before acquiring it, nor did I look any different. What did change markedly was how my friends treated me, not for the better, sad to say. I thought long and hard about the question of having money, because as I've said, I'd been down and out more than once. After due deliberation (and a couple of very nice holidays), the prospect of having a large bank account proved unimpressive to me. What's more, I found it made me lazy and complacent. In the end I found that, for me, having money was actually a detriment, not an asset, and I determined to be rid of it – ASAP!

That was not the difficult part, as you might imagine. Money is easy to be rid of, if that is your intention. After a few years of doing exactly as I pleased, with no yoke around my neck, I managed to accomplish my goal: I was once again without significant funds, and I had to figure out, once more, how to make a living. Even so, I felt a great weight lifted off my shoulders.

Ah, I can almost hear the chorus: "I'd be happy to give his situation a try!" But I assure you, I'm not lying, nor am I rationalizing poor financial decisions, nor would I take back the spending spree that landed me once more in the ranks of the so-called working class. In fact, I thank myself nearly every day that I threw that albatross off my neck – even when I'm broke and wondering how to pay the rent a few days out.

Many of us come from cultures where success is measured in terms of what we have, not necessarily who we are. I came to Corfu with very little money. I might have come sooner than I actually did, and had I done so I would have had substantial funds to last me a long time. But that's not how it happened. For some reason unknown to me at the time, I seemingly had to wait to do what I really wanted to do until I was financially least ready to do it. I could not take the easy road, so to speak, because what I really wanted, and probably what I really needed, was a challenge. Day-to-day challenge is what really turns my crank. I thrive on making something out of nothing. When I'm engaged, when I'm being of use, I feel great; when I'm lolling in affluence and being unproductive, I literally feel ill. Perhaps that is my strange little personality quirk, but I do recognize it for what it is, and I have learned to respect what my most basic nature keeps trying to tell me.

These days I live pretty much week by week, which seldom bothers me. I have not had a real holiday in years, which also seldom bothers me. I work very diligently every day, but I do not work to acquire money; I work simply to be of use. Of course everybody needs enough to get by, but if we stop to think about it, we probably need far less than we try to convince ourselves that we need. Some may say that money is the measure of accomplishment, and in our modern-day society that is at least partly true – but only partly. I much prefer the satisfaction of creating something that others appreciate to being able to buy the next widget. And to my great delight, I've found that the culture here on this beautiful little island in the Mediterranean seems to be concerned far less with what one has than it is about who one is. Is that some sort of irony, or did my subconscious know something all along? Did it steer me on this unlikely course simply to give me the opportunity for a major wake-up call? I can only smile and ponder such a notion.

As I write this account, the sum total of my wealth is measured in two figures. Not much money by today's standards. But I've been in worse straights, and I'm hardly worried, because I find that I am wealthy today in ways I was not even aware of previously. I am involved in a loving relationship (notice I did not say that I 'have' a loving relationship), I live in a beautiful place, among genuinely hospitable (and often charitable) people, I do good work (lots and lots of it), and I understand that chasing phantom redress is a not only a futile pursuit, it can sometimes be a downright denigrating one. What a lucky guy I am! I feel strong and secure. I am not afraid of the future. I can't wait to see what tomorrow might bring, and more importantly, what I might bring to it. I guess I'd call that a 'small fortune'!

FOUNTAIN OF YOUTH

Several hundred years ago Ponce de Leon was convinced he would find the legendary 'Fountain of Youth' somewhere in the American State of Florida. For anyone who has been to Florida (I have not), I'm sure they found plenty of nice beach towns and a fabulous theme park or two, but Ponce de Leon, during his time, found what was then an alligator infested swamp nearly the size of Great Britain. I'm sure it was a tremendous disappointment to him in his old age.

When I lived in the American State of Colorado, I was certain (or at least I was becoming convinced) that I would die a reasonably young man. I'd been plagued by chronic asthma for years, my blood pressure was consistently too high, and I contracted a whopping case of bronchitis every winter. In general, I felt less than vigorous, and I also had the sensation that I was losing ground with each passing year. Then I moved to Greece.

Within a few months of landing on Corfu, I began to have the ever-so-subtle yet unmistakable feeling that I was eating myself healthy again. My blood pressure dropped to normal and I subsequently tossed the tablets I was accustomed to taking daily into the trash. Likewise, my asthma disappeared and I stopped using my inhaler. I'd like to report that the gray hairs on my head began to disappear, and that the lines on my face began to smooth over as well, but that would be untrue. I did, however, begin to notice an uncharacteristic, healthy glow to my complexion.

Just a few years ago, statistics revealed that Greece had the third longest longevity rate in the world. At that time, only people living in certain parts of Japan and those living in the high Caucasus Mountains of Russia lived longer lives than the average Greek. Since I first became aware of that statistic, Greeks have slipped in their ranking a bit to number seven, which is still not bad. From personal observation, it did not take very long at all to realize that each time the church bell tolled in my village, it was for a man or woman well into their eighties or nineties. A bit more research, conducted by me just last summer, revealed that Greece is far down the list when it comes to the incidence of killing diseases such as cancer (all forms except brain cancer, in which Greece strangely ranks number one in the world). Go figure! I began asking some of my Greek friends why Greeks live so long, and the answers I received were simple and quite uniform. Firstly, I was told, the food eaten in Greece is simple and fresh; secondly, the people don't like to take pills. Good wholesome food, and no strange chemicals to corrupt the metabolism: makes perfect sense to me.

I've lived here on Corfu for more than seven years now, and from what I understand about human metabolism, it takes about seven years for every cell in the body to be replaced by new, fresher cells – nature's own fountain of youth, so to speak. If it's true that we are what we eat, then it follows that I've now become Greek (in the most organic sense). Which is just fine by me, as their track record concerning longevity is one to be emulated by most other peoples.

On my next birthday I will be fifty-seven years old, and I must report that I no longer envision myself leaving this world as a relatively young man. Of course, who knows what strange pranks fate holds in store? Still, I feel not only healthier than I did before coming here to live, but I also feel younger. Is it the food I eat? The air I breathe? Is it the fact that I've given up my car in favor biped transportation? Maybe it has something to do with my newfound one-day-at-a-time outlook on life. Who knows? It's probably a combination of all these factors. What I do know is that with the passing of each year, I feel more and more alive, and even though I know it can't happen, I feel as though I'm getting younger, not older. I feel like I'm going to live forever!

I can't help musing that I've somehow stumbled upon that illusive fountain that good old Ponce died trying to find. After all, it is here in Greece that the gods (mostly immortal) took corporeal form and chose to live. So who am I to argue? What surely must not be folly is the notion that attitude (as well as pure food and a clean environment) plays a major part in not only how long one lives, but how one lives; and whether I have fifty years or fifty days left on this planet, I've learned to deny the obvious. From my newfound perspective, Ponce de Leon was no fool; he was a visionary. He was simply looking on the wrong continent.

BIG FISH

The first summer that K. and I lived on Corfu, our friend Takis and his wife Lena took it upon themselves to show us many of the island's beaches. Each Sunday they arrived at our apartment around eleven in the morning ready for a daylong excursion. One Sunday we would head north, perhaps to Kassiopi, or San Stefanos; the next we would head south to Messonghi or Saint George. K. and I were grateful to our Greek friends for their hospitality, and we looked forward each Sunday to the outing.

After spending an hour or two swimming in the sea, we always indulged in a mid-afternoon repast. Sometimes we took a picnic lunch along, (which I liked best because Lena always cooked for all four of us and her Greek approach to a picnic was hardly sandwiches and potato chips, but rather roasted pork with roasted potatoes, *dolmades*, *taramousalada*, or other delightful treats); other times we ate at a beachside taverna (as a lifelong resident of Corfu, Takis knew where to find the best food at the cheapest prices). Going to the beach with Takis and Lena became a ritual that summer that K. and I will always remember fondly; that is, for the most part...

From past experience, I knew Takis to be both a fast and a voracious eater. (I once saw him devour nearly an entire lamb – organs, brain, ears, and eyeballs – in less than an hour.) Whenever we ate with Takis, his plate started out the fullest, and was empty first. For him, second helpings were a given, and often finished before we'd eaten our salad. Each time we had a meal with Takis, we rolled our eyes in amazement, not only by how much he ate, and how fast he cleared his plate, but that he managed to maintain a trim figure, even at age sixty-something!

One Sunday in late August of that year, Takis showed up as usual to collect us for the beach outing. K. and I never knew where he meant to take us on any given day, so we were prepared for anything – or so we thought. On this particular Sunday, rather than head straight for the highway as usual, Takis made a stop at a house in the hills just behind the village. As it turned out, the house was owned by his cousin Andreas from Athens, who, with his family, visited Corfu during the month of August each year. Apparently we were to have company on this week's excursion, which was fine with K. and me. A few words were exchanged between Takis and Andreas before Takis got back inside the car and drove out of the driveway. A few minutes later, we noticed that Andreas was following close behind in his car. "Where are we going this week?" I asked Takis. "Arillas," he told me. "Very nice beach; you will like it there!"

By the time we'd traveled into the mountains on our way to the northwest coast, it had become obvious to K. and me that we were not being followed by one car, but by a line of cars. I observed to Takis that it seemed as if others were following behind his cousin. "Other cousins," Takis explained succinctly, so K. and I now understood that we were included in some sort of annual family reunion.

Arriving in Arillas, we stopped first at a small fish taverna before heading to the beach. In turn, each car in the procession also stopped at the taverna, and before long no less than a dozen people, K. and myself included, were standing inside the restaurant's kitchen, examining freshly-caught fish. Shortly, a rather heated debate arose between Takis, his cousins, and the taverna's owner (twelve Greeks; thirteen opinions), as K. and I were left to wonder what the controversy was all about. But the debate seemed to finish as quickly as it had begun, and we were back inside the cars and headed for the shore before we knew it.

The beach at Arillas was just as Takis had promised it would be – cool, clear water with a shelf that went out more than a hundred meters. The water was bliss. Takis' cousins were quite amiable, even though none of them spoke English. After swimming, we all sunned ourselves on the beach. Takis and Lena engaged in conversation with their relatives, and K. and I felt fortunate to be included in the family gathering.

After an hour spent swimming and sunning, we moved to a small seaside taverna, where ouzo and *mezes* were ordered. The repast consisted of an array of small fishes: sardines, white bait, and others. The ouzo went down easily on a sunny afternoon, and K. and I were introduced to a variety of new tastes. Naturally, we figured that this was to be our lunch, so we ate and drank generously, if a little cautiously. Of course, we were wrong about the nature of the small feast: this was not to be lunch at all; it was merely a warm-up, so to speak. Lunch was yet to come.

Back at the taverna where we'd first stopped, the party of cousins (fifteen persons in all, including K. and me) settled themselves around a large table. The men stuffed napkins inside open shirt collars, as the women put aside their purses and prepared for the meal. Within minutes of our arrival, several pitchers of wine were brought to the table, as well as salad and the main course: a huge, open-mouthed fish that the men had apparently selected during our first visit earlier that morning.

Now, it is a given that various cultures have their differences concerning table manners, but K. and I were hardly prepared for the carnage that we were about to witness. The *Big Fish* was sectioned and served to each guest, but that is where all decorum seemed to end. Once on the plates of the Greek cousins, the Big Fish became fair game. Instead of forks and knives, fingers were the utensils of choice. Heads were bowed down, not in thankful prayer but in hunger, and within fifteen minutes the carcass was picked clean. Only the head and skeleton of the Big Fish remained. Apparently, Takis' well-known appetite was not his alone, but a family trait.

Well satisfied, the cousins sat back, sipped their wine, and chattered on and on in Greek. K. and I knew not what was being said, but it hardly mattered, as we'd been amazed into silence anyway by the utter voraciousness of these diners. Never before had we witnessed such an attack by humans upon a plateful of food. I looked over at K. and it was apparent that she was feeling a bit nauseous. I'd eaten quite sparingly (partly because I'd indulged in the extravagant *meze* earlier, and partly because I'd not been fast enough with my fork to get a fair share of the Big Fish), so I was spared the discomfort she was feeling, post feast!

Later, as we drove home through the mountains, Takis stopped the car and handed me the keys. "You drive!" he said. "I'm feeling too sleepy now." As I took the wheel, he sat in the back seat next to K. and fell asleep. The rest of the way home we listened to a litany of Takis' snoring and the Greek music that Lena, the channel flipper, found on the car radio.

And when we finally arrived home, K. and I tumbled out of the car and trudged up the steps to our apartment. Our faces were full of sun, and our stomachs bursting with the Big Fish. Even as we flopped down on our bed, arms wrapped round our stomachs, we knew not what to make of the bizarre spectacle we'd witnessed, though we did know that we would not need to eat again until the next Sunday.

A FADED PHOTOGRAPH

The first apartment that K. and I lived in after coming to Corfu was located in a very old building – one of Kontokali's oldest, I'm sure. Not that it looked all that different from the newer buildings that surrounded it, but there were a few telltale signs of its age. The staircase leading to the door was obviously hand-hewn (I am told that it has been designated as antique architecture and is therefore protected against demolition); the doors leading inside the apartment were obviously made decades ago, as the style is seen only on very old buildings in the Venetian Quarter of Corfu Town; and there was a water well located in the garden at the foot of the stairs, indicating that the building was in use long before city water had come to the village. Other signs of the buildings longevity were two-foot thick walls, a covered-over window in the bathroom where the outside wall of the adjacent building now stood, and creaky wooden floors (something not now seen since building codes prescribe pre-stress concrete framing as protection against earthquakes). I once asked my friend Takis, who was also my landlord, about the building's history, and he told me that as far as he knew, it was about two hundred fifty years old. He also told me that it was once the village bakery, and that his father had been the baker. The apartment itself was very, very hot in summertime, and K. and I often joked that the old bakery was still giving back the heat generated so long ago from the ovens.

The day we moved into the apartment was not the first time I'd seen the building. Nor was it the first time I'd slept there. On my very first visit to Corfu, I'd stayed in one of the building's other apartments for about ten days. That was in the early nineties. At that time, Takis' mother, Aphrodite, lived in the apartment that K. and I eventually occupied. On that first visit, Takis warned me about his mother, telling me that she was both senile and quite *xoxotropos*, meaning cantankerous. "You might hear her talking to herself," he warned. "Pay no attention to her."

By the time that K. and I moved into the apartment that was once Kontokali's bakery, and later Takis' mother's apartment, Aphrodite had passed away at the age of ninety-three. Little remained to remind us of her presence, or of her times, except a large, antique credenza that was obviously too heavy and too fragile to move down the narrow staircase. Arriving in Greece with little more than our clothes, K. and I were happy to have such a unique piece of furniture to use, and we polished the wood to a sheen not seen in decades.

We also painted the place from floor to ceiling, repaired cracked stucco, installed shelves and cabinets, replaced clouded glass, and made other cosmetic improvements. As the months passed, the venerable building became our home. Then one day I found an old faded photograph wedged behind one of the drawers of the credenza. The photo was of a middle-aged woman dressed from head to toe in black and standing at the foot of the very staircase that led to our apartment. The distant background in the photo also revealed that the building that now stood across the road had not existed at the time, and the view extended all the way to the sea. With a magnifying glass, I examined the face of the woman quite closely, and I soon became convinced that the face in the photo was a familiar one – a face not unlike that of my friend and landlord. I showed the photo to Takis, thinking that he might like to have it as a keepsake, but he only commented that the photo was of his mother, Aphrodite, and that it had probably been taken just after the war. He did not seem particularly interested in having the old photo, so I put it inside a book to keep it safe from moisture and dirt, and in time forgot about it altogether.

Some time later, I came upon the photo again. Feeling that it was a shame to hide it away, and also that such a venerable house deserved at least some acknowledgement of past inhabitants, I made a scan of the photo then restored it digitally as best I could, meaning to hang it above the doorway as a remembrance. The result of my effort was beyond all expectation and revealed details not seen in the original picture. Cast against the still-standing whitewashed staircase was not only Aphrodite's shadow, but a second one as well. I scrutinized the photo, trying to determine the source of the second shadow, but there was no one else in the picture to account for the second image. The phantom remained an anomaly.

Until, some time later, Takis and I got into a discussion about his boyhood in Kontokali, and about his family history. Aphrodite, I was told, had had a twin sister who had died as a child. On hearing such a revelation I at once thought about the faded photograph and about the mysterious second shadow.

I certainly do not profess to understand how such things happen, nor am I prepared to dismiss possibilities I cannot refute. I do know that the spirit of such ancient places reverberates still through the deeds and personalities of those long gone. As a result of seeing what I undeniably saw in the photograph, I have now come to see the cultural history of this village in the face of each villager. I suppose this is what today we call heredity. As for the second shadow, we do not now, nor may we ever, have an explanation for that.

STRANGE TALES FROM CORFU

Each year I live here in this tiny Greek village I seem to hear at least one really outlandish tale, sometimes macabre, but always off-the-charts weird. For example, one year a particularly gruesome story was going round about a white cargo van that stopped for innocent pedestrians walking alone at night along the road. Once inside the van, the unsuspecting walker was never seen again. Why? The rumor went that the occupants of the van were actually an ad hoc surgical team from Romania engaged in the illicit harvesting of organs (hearts, livers, kidneys) to steal and sell on the medical black market. Shivers! No wonder Mother told us not to accept rides from strangers!

A couple of years ago, my friend Rachel had taken a summer job as a waitress in Gouvia. Living at the time in Kontokali, she walked the short distance between villages each evening to the restaurant where she worked. Usually, she did not finish work until well after midnight. The road between the two villages is lined with homes and shops, and even at night it is fairly well traveled. Still, that did not stop the flasher who was lying in wait for her each night as she walked home from work. Night after night, from behind a different bush, or a dumpster, or a parked car, he would spring out at an unexpected moment and open his raincoat for Rachel to behold him in all his so-called glory. Rachel finally took to carrying a big rock with her, and one night she'd finally had enough of his antics and hurled the stone right at his privates. Now, you'd think that such a response would have discouraged the guy, but no! While he's not often seen (Ha!), once in a while the report of a sighting (Ha!) is heard to this day.

Then, of course, there is Kontokali's once-a-year strange death...

One year, a longtime resident of Gouvia Marina, Marcus by name, was seen drinking late into the evening at the Navigator's Bar. He left sometime before two o'clock in the morning, well soused, and was not seen again for days. When somebody finally went round to his boat to check on him, he was not there. The Good Samaritan took it upon himself to have a look around, but still found no trace of Marcus; not until, on leaving the boat, he noticed two shoes floating in the water just below the gangway, soles pointed up. On further inspection, he thought he saw a body floating upside-down in the murky water of the harbor. The police were summoned, who after investigating the Samaritan's claim, decided to employ a diver. The body was retrieved and identified as the missing Marcus. Apparently, on returning to his boat from the Navigator's that fateful night, he'd lost his footing on the gangway of his boat and fallen into the water, where he'd become entangled in ropes or rigging and drowned.

In an unrelated story, another longtime resident, a Dutchman named Jan, was a regular customer at one of the local pubs. He came often with his friend, another Dutchman called Uwe, to drink quietly together at a corner table. Neither of the men was particularly garrulous, and neither ever caused any trouble. One evening, the police visited the pub to enquire of the owner if he'd seen a Dutchman called Jan. As the twosome hadn't been to the pub in several days, the owner phoned Uwe, the friend. He'd not seen Jan either, so he went round to his house to check on him. Receiving no answer when he knocked on the door, he assumed that Jan had gone away for a few days. Back at the pub, however, Uwe related the story to the pub owner that for months Jan had spent most of his evenings either in the pub or at Uwe's house, telling his friend that he was afraid to go home at night because his house was full of ghosts; and, in fact, on the evening of his disappearance, he'd stayed at Uwe's place until the wee hours of the morning, terrified to go home. When Jan failed to turn up after more than a week, the police were called to his house to investigate. There they found the unfortunate Dutchman dead inside, his throat slashed from ear to ear. Gruesome! The pub owner is convinced (he told me so himself) that Jan's ghosts are responsible for the heinous act.

So, apparently Corfu can be a sinister place indeed after dark! Knowing what we know, and seeing what we've seen, many of us here listen with a perked ear to each strange sound after night has fallen, to each bump in the night. One never knows where danger lurks, or when his turn might come to enter the realm of Corfu's Dark Dreams...

WHAT'S SO GREAT ABOUT ENGLISH?

In a nutshell, what's so great about English is that nearly everybody speaks it these days!

That is certainly true here in Greece. In fact, shortly after I arrived here to live the Greek government passed a law declaring English as the country's official second language. What that means is that every school age child has at least some education in the English language. And as native English speakers either living in Greece or traveling frequently in Greece, what could be better? Especially since we (English and Americans and Canadians and Australians in particular) are so dedicated to our native tongue that we obstinately resist learning other languages. In fact, we sometimes become annoyed at others who do not speak English, no matter where they come from or what their native language might be. How tolerant we are in this regard!

Of course, American English is a derivative of the original, and it is often said that America and England are "two great countries separated by a common language." (Credit George Bernard Shaw.) For those of us hailing from the two different countries (so similar yet so very different culturally) it is easy to see not only the humor in that statement, but also its wisdom. Lucky for us, though, there is enough commonality between the two versions for us to get on quite well together, and even to share the nuances of our cultures in ways that those whose native tongue is different cannot – even if they speak English as a second language!

Nevertheless, the entire world, it seems, is dedicated to learning English. I must confess that I am continually amazed at the amount of English spoken here in Greece – and this is not a new phenomenon. Nearly twenty years ago, when I first began visiting Greece, it was true as well. In fact, I remember being so surprised by the amount of English spoken that I asked a young Greek woman who worked at the American Express office in Athens about it. She said: "We know the rest of the world is not going to learn Greek, so it is necessary that we speak English." Astute observation, considering it was twenty years ago. And it is no less true today. The Greeks (as well as just about everyone else who comes from a small country that speaks its own language) understand that English has become the world's first universal language, and prefer it or not, they certainly embrace it. Again, how lucky for those of us who learned English at our mother's breast!

Frankly, I love the English language. It is a rich one indeed, with a huge vocabulary, countless idioms, interesting dialects, and often a humorous perspective. I have even chosen to make my living (more or less) conveying ideas in the English language. I owe it a lot.

I must also now state, for the record, that I am not one of those who refuse to learn other languages. I speak good conversational German (the language from which English is derived; it's true), reasonable street French, and an ever increasing amount of Greek (which I have learned by necessity rather than by choice). Still, I'm constantly encountering English-speaking people who live year round here in Greece, people who have lived here longer than I, who obstinately refuse to learn even the most basic phrases in Greek. Usually, these people become irritated when they do encounter a Greek that doesn't speak English (as if English had been ordained by God Almighty as the only civilized tongue on the planet). I'm certainly not ready to make that assumption, but the rapid spread of English not only throughout Europe, but also across the globe, suggests that before long nearly everyone will speak it, at least to some degree.

Recalcitrant attitudes aside, I do have one story to relate that poignantly demonstrates the commitment of the Greeks to learn English, even as it demonstrates my own rather feeble effort to bridge the so-called language gap – or at least what's left of it – which isn't much! During our second winter here on Corfu, a young woman who owned and operated the *frontestirio* in our village approached K. and I with a proposition. (For those who do not know, a *frontestirio* is a secondary school that most Greek children attend after the finish of their regular classes at school. The purpose of most *frontestirios* is the teaching of foreign language, predominantly, though not exclusively, English.) The young woman proposed to K. and me that we become teachers at her language school, the reason being that: 1) she was short of teachers; and 2) she felt her students needed the experience of being taught by native speakers of the language. We were flattered by her offer, but not speaking much Greek we were also skeptical of our ability to teach English to Greek-speaking children. The teacher told us not to worry, because her technique was one of total immersion; namely, only English was spoken in the classroom, even to the youngest students, who were all of nine or ten years old. After a number of attempts, she persuaded us to give it a try; K. would teach the younger children, and I would teach the older ones.

For a period of two months, we visited the school regularly to gain a sense of the instructional system being employed, as well as to meet the students: to see the place in action, so to speak. These visits only fed our initial skepticism, but the young and friendly teacher remained convinced that we were indeed the ones for the job, and she dismissed our objections one after another and cajoled us to continue. Eventually, both K. and I did indeed head various classes. The instruction technique was, to say the least, rigorous. The younger students were wildly enthusiastic, but also quite unruly. The older ones already spoke a good deal of English and often amazed me by their knowledge of what I would have considered sophisticated words and phrases. The teacher, we soon learned, had done her job well. Whether or not we were doing her effort justice remained, for us, quite in question.

After two months at the *frontestirio*, both K. and I decided that the job was quite beyond us. Not that we were deficient in our language skills, but we felt decidedly inept as teachers. With our apologies and our thanks to our benefactor, we resigned the ad hoc post, leaving the instruction of English in the hands of those more capable than us – namely Greek teachers who had been trained (mostly in the UK) to teach the English language.

I might say that it was a humbling experience for us, but that would be understating the truth. In fact, we both gained great respect for both the teachers and the students at the *frontestirio*. Their dedication went far beyond anything either of us had ever seen in American schools, and we presumed that the same might hold true for English schools. Apparently, the pressing need to learn a subject tends to generate such overwhelming enthusiasm, but of course we who speak English shall never know about that need, shall we? Which makes me ask the question: Are we indeed the lucky ones?

David A. Ross

SPEAKING AMERICAN

One of the predominant reasons that K. and I chose Corfu, and particularly Kontokali, as our new home when we decided to leave the States and live in Europe was the fact that we were well aware that there was a large British community of ex-pats already living here. We reasoned that such a community would cushion the blow of moving to a place where English was not the native language, and certainly we were right. Not only did the British community here speak our language (at least in theory) but also their culture was somewhat similar to our own. To our delight, the Brits living here on Corfu welcomed us with open arms, including us not only in their community, but also in their cultural rituals; and for their openness and acceptance we will always be grateful.

In the beginning, however, we were often chided (always good-naturedly) not only for our accents, but also for our curious (to them) colloquialisms. Over time, of course, they became accustomed to our way of speaking, as did we to theirs. Recently, however, I received and e-mail from another American calling me to task for my 'English usage'. Here is that e-mail:

"David! My only confrere on this Board! You have been hanging around too many Brits! "That's not what we're on about"??? Hmmm... Me thinks you need some Yanks to hang with, mate!"

As writers, both K. and I value deeply the richness of our native language; and while there are many not-so-significant differences between British English and the American version, communication is always effortless and fruitful. Having not been back to the States in almost eight years, I must confess that I'm not exactly up to date on my American slang. This is borne out by the American television shows I occasionally see on the Greek channels. A couple of years ago K. went back to the States for a visit with her family, and while she'd certainly not lost her ability to communicate effectively, she did notice a few gaps in her awareness of certain 'new' colloquialisms. Speaking English (or American English) in a foreign culture, one learns to speak not only slowly, but also very precisely, particularly to those to whom English is not their native tongue. We often use the simplest words to make ourselves understood, and we certainly refrain from using the slang expressions so prevalent in our own culture. Talking every day with Brits, a certain amount of the British vernacular has admittedly seeped into our conversation (as evidenced by my quite unconscious expression which was pointed out in the recent e-mail). These days we routinely use such expressions as "Having a go at" or "going on about". These are decidedly not American expressions, rather they are colloquialisms we've picked up from the Brits since living here on Corfu. Not to mention various Greek expressions, as well, that have become part of our daily conversations: *"Tipota"*; *"etsy-ketsy"*, *"Po, po, po"*, and others.

Recently I watched a bit of the MTV Music Awards on TV. The event was held in LA (which is, ironically, where the woman who sent me the e-mail lives) and the language I was hearing from the 'presenters', I must admit, baffled me. Even as the Hip-hop culture has permeated the rest of the world (at least in the media) the 'lingo', I must confess, eludes me. Apparently, I am now a 'stranger living in a strange land'.

Just as in England, various dialects are spoken in different parts of America – (Oops! There's another one: in the States we never refer to our country as America, rather as the United States, or the US, or simple 'the country', and isn't that obtuse), and I sometimes found, even while living there, that I had difficulty understanding those dialects. I recall being in the Boston airport, for example, and finding it nearly impossible to understand the announcements being broadcast(ed) over the PA. (Do Brits use that term: *PA*? In American English, it stands for Public Address). An even more dramatic example of my now curtailed understanding of 'Americanese' was made evident when Hurricane Katrina struck New Orleans. Listening to interviews with the many Black Americans stranded in the city, I found I often knew even less about what was taking place than I had before hearing their accounts. American talk shows, like Oprah and Jon Stewart's Daily Show, both of which are aired on Greek TV (albeit at odd hours), are another reminder that I am indeed far, far away, and a bit out of touch.

No matter... Or, as they say here in Greece: "*Then peraza!*" The main thing is that I (we) are able to communicate reasonably well, and perhaps our ignorance of modern-day American colloquialisms is even a blessing, as it forces us to use our native language in its 'purest' form. Though I suspect, that were I to sit down with an American, in America, for an extended conversation, then a few curious nuances in my current vocabulary might become obvious.

What can I say? In the end we are all quite adaptable, and we copy what we see and hear as if we were monkeys, not humans. No apologies mate. As Pop-eye the Sailor was known to say: "I am what I am, and that's all that I am..."

THE MANY OF VARIED
MISADVENTURES OF FELIX THE CAT

In Greece, a cat is considered by many to be a garden animal, much as a squirrel or chipmunk is regarded in Britain or America. Most cats are left to fend for themselves, the thinking being that they will control the rodent population more effectively if they must hunt for their food. The average life expectancy for an outdoor cat in Greece, I'm told by a veterinarian, is about three years. This is due to the many hazards they encounter (mainly car traffic) as they prowl through village alleyways, congregate in front of restaurants, or explore the countryside unprotected.

K. and I adopted our cat Felix from an animal shelter about a year before we came to Greece to live. At the time it was assumed that he was about three years old, but his actual history was unknown. Over time we have concluded that he'd been brought to the shelter after his original owner had died. (We have our reasons for making this assumption.)

For the first year that Felix was with us, we lived in a

city apartment, so he remained an indoor cat. He seemed happy enough with the arrangement, so we naturally assumed that that had been his previous lifestyle as well. When we decided to come to Corfu to live, the question obviously arose about what to do with Felix. Even during the first year he'd lived with us, we'd grown quite fond of him, and we really did not want to give him up. At the same time, the thought of moving an animal five thousand miles to a new home on a different continent seemed to us a bit far-fetched. Finally, we made the difficult decision to give him up, and K. found a very nice fellow who agreed to adopt him. Arrangements were made, and on a Saturday morning one week before we were to leave for Greece, the new caretaker arrived to collect him. After a short bonding session, and a tearful good-bye, Felix was off to his new home. Or so we thought...

As the hours passed that day, K. grew more and more despondent about giving Felix up for adoption; and about seven that evening she decided to telephone the new owner to see what might be arranged concerning his return. "I've made the biggest mistake," she told the fellow. "I've given away my best friend." Well, it's easy to say in hindsight that Felix had worked his way deep into her heart, and the decision was made to take him to Greece, come what may. We telephoned the airline and bought his passage from Denver to Frankfurt, then on to Athens.

Felix made the journey to Greece like a real trooper. Inside his flexible carrier bag, he flew underneath the forward seat for fourteen hours without making a sound (somewhat uncharacteristic; he's normally quite a talker, which he probably gets from me) and without making a mess (if you get my drift).

Once we'd moved into our new digs on Corfu, Felix seemed to make the adjustment without concern. He was still an indoor cat, as he'd never known anything else; but when we'd return after being out, we'd see his little head looking through the parted shutters of our kitchen window, and I began to wonder just how long we could keep him inside our small apartment before he grew curious and ventured out on his own. We decided to introduce him to the great outdoors of our small garden, and of course his new outdoor life was soon underway.

As that first summer grew hotter and hotter, we of course left our windows open, and Felix soon determined that the open window just above the stairs leading to the garden was his doorway. He came and went at will, and sometimes he was gone for hours. Yet he always returned, sometimes with a gift for us.

As autumn came and the nights grew colder, Felix became an avid hunter. Not only did he leave mice he'd caught on our windowsill, he picked bats right out of the air in mid-flight and deposited them in our small lounge. As cats will be, he was immensely proud of his conquests. One night, I got up in the middle of the night to find a very large (and very dead) rat deposited smack in the center of our lounge. All in a night's work for Felix!

I was personally quite happy Felix had attained his freedom to come and go at will, and to do as cats do outdoors. He seemed very happy with the new arrangement, and obviously there was a vast world beyond our walls for him to explore. All seemed to be going quite well until one day he went outside in the early morning but failed to return by ten that evening. Needless to say, we were worried for his safety and went round the immediate environment looking for him. We found no trace of him, nor did he return that night. Next day, we searched the village, but of course finding a cat that does not wish to be found is next to impossible. He did not return on that second day, or the next. We posted his photo around the village, along with a message that said he was missing, as well as our contact information. For nine days we neither saw him nor heard any information that might determine what had happened to him. I admit that I thought the worst, that he'd wandered out to the highway and been struck by a car, then his remains disposed of by whomever. K. remained more optimistic. "I know he's not dead," she maintained. "I'm just afraid that he's been injured and is unable to come home."

Just when we'd really come round to giving him up for lost, K. heard our neighbor calling to her. "K.! K.! *Gato*! *Gato*!" We rushed down to the garden to find Felix, emaciated and a bit delirious (or so it seemed). Wherever he'd been for the past ten days, it was obvious that he'd not had food, and probably little to drink. We brought him inside our apartment, but he was so bad off that he did not even seem to recognize that he'd come home. He crouched underneath our desk, barely moving, and I was afraid he would not last the night. We telephoned a vet, who said he would come after four hours. When the vet arrived, he too was skeptical about Felix's recovery. He gave him a shot of Cortisone to help him breathe, and also to ease whatever pain he might have been experiencing. "He's obviously starving," said the vet. "If he'll take food and water, there's a chance, but we'll just have to wait and see." When the vet left, I was able to coax him to take a few bites of tuna, though I was still fearful that he was on his last legs, so to speak.

That night we took turns sitting up with him. When morning came, he was still with us, though very, very weak. His back legs would barely carry his weight, and it was heartbreaking to see him try to walk, only to falter and fall down. For two straight weeks we fed him better than we fed ourselves, giving him an entire roasted chicken, tuna fish, pork chops, steak, and whatever else we thought might nourish him back to health. Slowly, he began to regain his strength, though it took several months before he was able to use his hind legs to even jump the short distance from the floor onto our bed.

Another time, he managed to get some sort of wild reed inside his eye, and we had to have the vet perform surgery to remove it. "This plant is particularly dangerous for cats," Dr. Markos told us, "because it grows into their system and entangles itself around the heart."

Sometime later, Felix was attacked by a fox, required two separate surgeries, and spent the next three months gaining back the use of one of his hind legs.

The apartment where we now live is two and a half stories above the street. It has three balconies. Felix likes to walk the railings, fearless and indignant as a circus performer, and does not seem very concerned that there is no net below to catch him if he falls. And fall he has – twice!

These days, Felix has gone into voluntary retirement. He seldom goes outside, and when he does, it is only to sniff around the garden. Unlike his more independent youth, he always comes home when we call him. He's nearly twelve years old now, after all, and he's earned his leisure. He still walks the railings though; there seems to be no way to stop him. By Greek standards, he is a very old cat. By my calculation, he's used up eight of his nine lives. He's durable if nothing else. We still take great enjoyment from his company, and it seems that the feeling is mutual. We're hoping that his so-called retirement will mean no more mishaps, but perhaps that is too much to assume. Until Felix's next great misadventure, we bide our time. This morning, as I write, he's camped out on top of the bookcase, which means he's about to take yet another nap. I can relax, knowing he's safe and sound. But I often wonder: Just when and how did I become so devoted a pet owner? And aside from that, who actually owns whom? It's a question that every cat owner must face sooner or later.

A MYSTERIOUS KEY

On a cold and rainy afternoon in mid-December 2004, K. and I wandered into the Navigator's Pub in Kontokali for a glass of wine and a little company. Finding our good friend Phil there, we joined him at a table near the fireplace and ordered our drinks.

We particularly like going to this pub on rainy winter afternoons because it is warm and intimate. Many of the village locals pass their winter afternoons there, as well as a few Greeks, because it breaks up the monotony of those seemingly endless gray winter days. This day seemed no different than others we'd spent their, swapping stories, complaining about the weather, and about leaky roofs, or telling a few jokes.

Not long after we'd arrived, the owner of the pub came up to us and handed us a piece of paper rolled up into a cylinder and tied closed with a blue ribbon. He handed one to Phil as well. "What's this?" we asked, and, with a cat-who-ate-the-mouse look on his face, he said he was not at liberty to say. "Should we open it?" we asked, and he nodded as he turned and walked back to the bar.

K. unfastened the ribbon, as did Phil with his scroll,

and each began to read the message inside. "What is it?" I asked.

"It's an invitation," she said. "And there's a key inside."

"What sort of invitation?" I asked.

"It's to a party," she said, holding up the key.

I looked questioningly at Phil, as I knew him to be a notorious prankster. "Did you have something to do with this?" I asked. He assured me that he did not, and that his invitation was the same as ours. He held up his key and shrugged his shoulders. The invitation read: "Your presence is kindly requested at the Navigator's Pub on 27 December, 2004 at nine o'clock sharp. Dress is to be festive."

I looked first at Phil, then at K.. We were each at a loss concerning the curious invitation as it had defined neither the occasion we would apparently be marking, nor who had sent out the summons. What the mysterious key might open, we had no clue.

On the appointed evening, still quite in the dark as to what we might be in for, K. and I presented ourselves at the Navigator's at the appropriate time. Of course we'd engaged in endless speculation during the two weeks prior as to what might be in store for us, as well as from whom the invitation had come. We knew that Phil had also received an invitation, but we knew of no one else who had, and the key remained the biggest mystery of all.

When we arrived at the Navigator's, the owner seated us at a long table set for eight. K. and I were apparently the first to arrive, so we sat alone and speculated that the whole thing might just be some elaborate hoax played upon us by Phil, but that notion was quickly dispelled when Phil came through the door looking more dapper than we'd ever seen him look. Within a few moments, others arrived for the soiree, some of whom we knew casually, and others we did not know at all. Everyone seated at the table held an invitation identical to the one we'd received, and nobody seemed to know just what mystery the eight silver keys might unlock.

Within minutes of the arrival of the last guest, an array of appetizers was brought to table, and several pitchers of wine, as well. Speculation about what all this might mean replaced more normal conversation, and if anyone at the table knew anything, they certainly weren't inclined to give away the secret.

After about forty-five minutes, the owner of the pub began clearing away plates and glasses and announced to us that we had to leave the pub at once. We were all a bit flabbergasted by his command, and K. said, "I guess this is good-bye; we're being barred, though I can't imagine why."

"All of us?" I said. "That doesn't make sense. Why would we be barred? We haven't done anything to offend."

Then the owner informed us that there were three taxis waiting out in the road to take us to our destination, and that we should proceed at once to the cars. We all looked at one another skeptically, but reasoned, 'In for a penny, in for a pound!' K. and I piled into the lead car and watched as others occupied the two other taxis for a ride to who-knew-where. A moment later, we were speeding out of the village and into the mountains.

After a twenty-minute ride along a dark and ever-ascending highway, the car stopped in front of an old stone house. We got out and waited in the chilly night air for the others to arrive. Within five minutes' time, the other two cars arrived as well, and all eight of us stood in front of the stone house wondering what was to come next.

After a very indecisive moment, a man appeared at the door to the house and invited us all to come inside. Crossing the threshold, an intimate taverna was revealed, and we were seated at a table near the roaring fireplace. Still, we had no idea where we were or what was up.

Finally, one of the women in the group revealed the purpose of the gathering. "We are all here tonight to celebrate Jon Spate's seventy-fifth birthday!" Delores Spate announced. Her husband Jon seemed as surprised as the rest of us.

Like whirling dervishes, three waiters descended upon our table, laying more food and popping open several bottles of champagne. "Everyone enjoy!" said Delores.

After several toasts had been made to Jon, more food arrived. Glasses clinked, music played, conversations bubbled. "What an outrageous idea!" said Janine, one of the guests.

As the evening progressed, more and more food was brought to the table: an array of a dozen or more appetizers, followed by filet mignon, followed by a truly decadent birthday cake. All the while, pitcher after pitcher of wine was brought to the table, followed by after dinner cognac. Finally, somebody asked the inevitable question: "What do the keys open, Delores?"

Delores only smiled. "My husband Jon has lived seventy-five glorious years," she said. "His life has been rich with good friends and full with experience. The keys open the door to each of your futures. May your time be as rewarding as Jon's has been!"

We were stunned into silence. What a grand gesture she had made to commemorate her husband's seventy-fifth birthday, and indeed to pay tribute to his life! We all raised our glasses to Jon for yet another toast, but each of us knew that we were not only toasting Jon's life, but our own as well. At that moment, we were each keenly aware of the force behind our own existence, and we were, in turn, each opening the door to our future.

When the grand repast finally finished well past three o'clock in the morning, the taxis were waiting outside to take each of us wherever we desired. As K. and I sped home in the back seat of the taxi, we were each quietly aware of our greater destination. Special thanks to Delores Spate, who showed us all a glimpse of our own destiny, and our endless possibilities, even as she paid tribute to the man she loved.

David A. Ross

MEDITERRANEAN LUNCH

A couple of days ago my wife and I were fortunate enough to partake in a ritual that seems to be practiced to perfection in this part of the world – a ritual that I call the "Mediterranean Lunch".

In order to engage in this so-called ritual properly, one must first have at least three hours to kill. That is essential, because the Mediterranean lunch embodies far more than one's midday repast. It is also a time of pure idleness, a time for conversation, or daydreaming.

To my mind, there are certain rules for engaging in a proper Mediterranean lunch. First, the meal must be taken in a shady location, preferably outdoors, weather permitting. Secondly, it should be taken in several slow courses, beginning with wine (or the libation of one's choice, but wine is preferable), and followed by a somewhat frivolous appetizer. When the waiter asks whether or not you intend to order a main course, he should be dismissed at least once, so that more time can be spent in conversation or simply looking over the environment. Once the wine has been drunk, and the appetizer eaten, it is acceptable to order the main course.

The lunch itself should consist of salad (because local Mediterranean produce is always fresh and renewing), and should then be followed by fish, or pasta, or perhaps a sandwich, but only if the sandwich is made on a baguette, or *ciabata*, or pita bread. Of course, a second carafe of wine should be ordered with the meal.

Once the food is brought to table, it should be eaten slowly, reflectively, taking plenty of time to comment upon the scenery, or upon some other mundane subject. Nothing too heavy will do during this conversation, because it is essential that a tranquil and balanced attitude be maintained during the repast (for the sake of digestion).

After the main course has been eaten and the plates cleared away, it is then time for yet another pause, perhaps for a cigarette, if one smokes, or maybe for a trip to the facilities. A bit more musing is always acceptable, for there is no hurry to be anywhere else.

After an acceptable amount of time has passed, it is essential that a decadent dessert be ordered, preferably something containing copious amounts of chocolate, or perhaps something smothered in a liqueur. At our recent Mediterranean lunch, we ordered a crepe drenched in chocolate augmented with banana and ice cream. It is acceptable to share the dessert amongst two people. It is also best to order coffee along with the dessert – not watery Nescafe, but the real thing – espresso or cappuccino, or the like.

Following dessert, it is also essential to allow time for digestion. Remember, there is no hurry to pay one's bill. All in good time!

Lastly, when one finally leaves the restaurant (and it is assumed that at least three hours have passed), a short walk in scenic surroundings is advised. But only a short walk! After two carafes of wine, one's legs might feel a bit heavy, not to mention one's eyelids. So, of course, the final stage of this time honored ritual is a late afternoon nap.

I am not privileged enough to partake in the ritual of

the Mediterranean Lunch all that often, but when I do, I practice it to perfection, as it is a short holiday in an otherwise busy life.

IT'S NOT EASY BEING GREEN

Here we are on the 'Emerald Isle'. Have you ever seen this place from the air? It does indeed look like an emerald upon a marine blue setting. The vision is a stunning one that will not soon be forgotten by one who sees it. My friend Takis has told me that he is convinced that Corfu is a gift from the gods, and I think he must be right.

Unlike other Greek islands, Corfu is a veritable garden. Virtually anything will grow here – leafy trees, ferns, succulents, palms, cacti, fruits and vegetables. In winter, the oranges on the orange trees are so prolific that at least half are never harvested and fall to the ground, uneaten. What a cornucopia we have here on the 'Emerald Isle'.

And our ecological good fortune here is not confined to the fauna. We have an abundance of clean water (albeit a bit salty and heavy with minerals), and the air is still pristine ninety-nine percent of the time. The late oceanographer Jacque Cousteau said that the waters of the Adriatic and the Ionian Seas were the cleanest on the planet. Good food, fresh air, clean water – the most basic essentials of a good life – we are blessed to have an abundance here. How lucky we are!

Still, I've wondered from time to time just where all the garbage we create goes here on Corfu...

I asked some questions of locals and longtime residents, and it turns out that there is indeed a landfill here on Corfu. Makes sense, I guess. I know how much refuse is created every day in my house, and surely it must be likewise in other homes. Of course, the landfill is well out of sight (after all, this is a tourist destination, and it would hardly do to have visitors passing by such an eyesore). In fact, I've never seen it, I do not really know where the garbage I create ends up, or how it is treated. And isn't that the case for most of us, no matter where we live.

Another issue I've begun thinking about is the energy we use. Here on Corfu we have no rivers, therefore no hydroelectric power can be produced. Neither have we coal to burn, nor is there natural gas. (Here it comes in pressurized bottles bought at any local mini-market). We certainly do not have a nuclear facility here to produce electricity, so judging from the heftiness of my electric bills I can only assume that the power must be purchased from other sources.

These days, as I look at the prolific greenery that surrounds me, I am much more ecologically aware than I once was; it seems only natural, living here in the garden...

For example, I try to buy locally grown vegetables whenever possible. Not only are they fresher, but also because there is no need to transport them thousands of kilometers, thereby using petrol and fouling the environment. In my former life in America, I used to drive a car; here I ride a pushbike. I've come to understand that modern-day packaging of just about everything is an ecological abomination, so I try as best I can to avoid contributing to the overwhelming refuse created by vacuum seals and plastic carrier sacks. Admittedly, my effort is a small one, and certainly far less than is needed. I know I could and should do better. Even a dog will not foul his own den.

Recently I was reading an article written by Al Gore, the man who by all rights should have been President of the United States had democracy actually prevailed in my home country, and I learned a few rather alarming facts concerning the environment that support all life on this fragile planet, this oasis in space, this terrain we so carelessly defile.

Mr. Gore reminds us that, "while the climate crisis on our planet may appear to be happening slowly, it is in fact a true planetary emergency. Voluminous scientific evidence exists that suggests strongly that, unless we each act quickly and decisively to deal with the causes of global warming, our world will likely experience a string of catastrophes.

"Apparently, "we are melting virtually all the mountain glaciers in the world--including those of the Rockies, the Sierras, the Andes, and the Alps, and, more ominously, the massive ice field on the roof of the world, on the enormous Tibetan Plateau, which has 100 times more ice than the Alps, and which supplies up to half the drinking water for up to 40 per cent of the world's people, through seven river systems that originate there: the Indus, the Ganges, the Brahmaputra, the Salween, the Mekong, the Yangtze, and the Yellow. Even more important, we are rapidly melting the vast, but relatively thin, floating ice cap that covers the Arctic Ocean."

And that's not all that Mr. Gore, and others, have to say on the subject. In fact, many believe that the grandchildren of the present generation may not inherit a planet where life is sustainable, as we know it today. That's what I call 'Big News.'

Yet, many governments, while paying such claims (and such evidence) lip service, do little to impact the situation that we have all created in little more than a century. With such a lack of insight, and even less leadership, it must fall upon us as citizens of this fragile planet to do what we can, to 'live simply that others may simply live.' The task is daunting, and the consequences of past actions perhaps unavoidable, but I, for one, living here on this oasis in the Med, in this proverbial garden, shall continue to do my small part, and I shall try to improve upon my more deleterious ecological habits as well. In the face of all evidence, there seems little else to do, for the time has come for the gluttony and the ecological destruction to end.

In truth, this issue is the greatest ever to face not only our species, but each and every species on Earth. It must take precedence over the petty religious and political and racial wars in which we involve ourselves, wars that our so-called leaders tell us are imperative that we win to save our cultures, yet without the basics for sustenance, such claims seem to me to be all the more hollow. Indeed, had Mr. Gore been given his due, there would most probably be no "War on Terror", but instead a dramatic effort toward putting right an environment that we have so thoughtlessly endangered.

More and more, it seems to me, that the right man seldom is granted our permission to act decisively on our behalf. Instead, we tend to bow to power groups, and their selfish and nefarious agendas may well prove to be our legacy as a species. Why do we do so?

I willingly admit that I do not do enough to preserve the fragile ecological balance that sustains me (and my kind). I need to do better. We all need to wake up before it's too late, and to insist that our leaders do so as well. But even more important, we must act responsibly day-to-day. Find out where your garbage goes, and how it is treated. Demand alternative energy sources to power your homes, your cars, your commercial establishments, and your factories. It's not easy being green, but let's all remember that the alternative is being barren. Which inevitably leads to EXTINCTION.

WILL THEY EVER LEARN

One morning a couple of years ago I was sitting on the patio at my favorite breakfast café having my usual morning cappuccino when I met a young (early to mid-forties I would guess) Englishman who had just come from the airport and was waiting there for a ride. We began to talk, as people do, and I learned that it was his first visit to Corfu, though his wife had come here some years before and had always wanted to return. I also learned that he owned a very successful pub quite near one of the major airports in the UK, and that he had a teenage son. We talked about a number of other things as well, and he seemed quite interested about my life here on Corfu. After another coffee, his ride eventually showed up, and we bid one another good-bye. It was an experience not unlike a hundred others I'd had, so I did not think much more about it.

Until the next winter, when one very rainy day I saw him on the street very near the café where we'd first met. I approached him to say hello, and indeed he remembered me too. He told me that he'd come to Corfu this time with his family, that they meant to find a place to live, as well as a vacant bar to rent where he could start a business. Trying to be both sociable and encouraging, I invited him and his family to dinner at my apartment that night. He accepted, and the date was made.

When they arrived for dinner, I met his wife and his son. They all seemed like nice enough people as we talked mostly about their plans for living on Corfu. I tried to impart a bit of my newfound knowledge about island living in Greece, but mostly they wanted to talk about their own plans, so I left them to it.

Apparently, they were in the process of selling both their home and their business in the UK. Corfu had been the wife's dream for years, and they meant to make it their permanent home. They made a point of telling me how well prepared they were for the move – especially financially! And compared with my meager existence it did indeed seem to me that they meant to import a good bit of money into the local economy. I remember trying to tell them to be careful, that Corfu had its particular way of picking pockets clean, but I was reassured that they were wise to the ways of the world, and that I had no cause to worry about them. They knew exactly what they were doing, and they seemed convinced that no matter what obstacle might present itself, having enough money would solve the problem. Since I've learned over the years that it's rather futile to talk to a brick wall, I shut my mouth and just listened as they went on and on about their plans.

The couple did indeed find a house, as well as a vacant bar to rent. I never visited the house, but I heard all about it. It sounded large and somewhat luxurious, at least by Corfu's standards. As the bar was in the village where I live, I was able to watch from afar as they began to renovate the place they intended to open in spring.

Well, the bar never opened due to some dispute with the landlord. But that did not deter this couple. For the next year I saw them from time to time, usually in a restaurant or a bar, relaxing and apparently having a good time. It appeared that they had not exaggerated their financial position, as money seemed not to be a deterrent to having fun on Corfu.

Eighteen months later (it was just before Christmas, I remember) I again encountered the man, this time on the boat of my friend. He looked quite obviously down in the mouth, not to mention desperate. He told me that his marriage had fallen apart and that his wife had gone back to the UK. He and his son had given up the luxurious house they'd rented some months before and were now living in a small apartment without proper heating. That day he'd walked five miles from where they were living to try to find a bit of work so he could buy food. The rent was coming due at the first of the month and he had no idea how he would pay for a roof over their heads. And, by the way, did I have any spare change for a bus ride home?

By springtime, the man and his son were having a tabletop sale to be rid of the last of their possessions, acquiring enough money for two plane tickets home being their less than auspicious goal. Apparently they raised the needed money, because I've not seen them since that day.

Each spring, it seems, I invariably encounter someone much like the couple I describe. I hear the story of how they've sold out in the UK and mean to make a life here on Corfu. Without exception, these people boast a bit about their current state of financial affairs, and without exception they believe that simply having enough money will see them through any problem they might encounter along the way. Their futures look rosy, the possibilities seem endless. Nothing will stand in the way of their dream.

Two years ago it was a couple that rented out a vacant restaurant/bar that has literally had a curse upon it for years – a place where business after business has failed due to poor location. Like the others, they sunk their fortune into the place, and they were closed before the finish of September, disgusted and broke. Trying to hang on to their grand vision, they did not leave Corfu, and the last I saw them was in December when they showed up at my place to borrow fifty euros – for food.

Last year it was a single woman from Wales. She made no secret of the fact that she had a small fortune, and that she meant to spend it. The vultures circled as if she were nearly dead in the desert. This case was particularly disturbing, because the woman managed to go through a quarter million pounds in the short period of four months. She, too, is now back in the UK, though rumor has it that she's coming back to initiate lawsuits to get her money back. I can't help thinking that whatever resources she might still have will be at risk. Corfu has a way of emptying one's pockets before he knows what has happened. Some people never learn.

Since Corfu is a small place, and each village is a micro-society unto itself, people are bound to talk. There are few secrets here, especially when it comes to the ex-pats. Cough at one end of the village and someone on the opposite side will enquire how your pneumonia is coming along. One night in a restaurant I engaged another longtime ex-pat in a discussion about the phenomenon of British refugees who come to Corfu with a pile of money and end up leaving in dire straights. My conversation partner (who was himself British, and no youngster) offered an interesting perspective. In his opinion, he told me, it was far better to arrive on Corfu with fifty pounds in your pocket than with your life savings on the line; because if one arrived with very little, of course he had little at risk (which would inevitably fall into the hands of sharks). And if one arrived with not much more than the clothes on his back, then he would be obliged to take this new society on its own terms.

What my friend was saying seems all too apparent to me, but to many, they must necessarily import the ideas and standards of the culture from which they came, ideas and standards that never prove true here. Those of us who have managed to find a way to exist here can spot these so-called pigeons a mile away. We can smell it in the air even before they've arrived, even before they start flashing their money like a diamond in the Mediterranean sun. We shake our heads. We gossip a bit. We make bets on how long it will take before they're up to their necks in trouble and on the plane bound for home. It's a sad situation, really.

But I'm sure that next spring I'll see the scenario played out yet again. One can't offer a warning – this much I've learned. A know-it-all with money in his pocket is the smartest person yet born, and no matter what one might say, in the end he will bend the situation to his own advantage. You can bet on that! Money talks, they'll tell you. Of course, in the end it is the quiet ones hiding their fangs that end up with full pockets.

A WEDDING, A FUNERAL
AND A FESTIVAL

K. and I had lived on Corfu more than four years before we were invited to our first Greek wedding. Harry, the son of our friend Spiros, was getting married to Joanna, a girl from Cyprus. The wedding ceremony was to be at 6:00 p.m. at the church in Kontokali; the reception was schedule for 8:00 o'clock that evening. Nearly everyone in our village was invited.

Arriving at the church at the appointed hour, we found a crowd of people gathered in the street. Apparently, the small chapel was already filled to capacity, but a loudspeaker system was in place so that those of us that had to stand outside could hear the ceremony. Being that it was spring, the rain started just as the ceremony began, but it did not deter those standing in the street. Taking cover beneath umbrellas, we braved the rain to hear the priest pronounce Harry and Joanna man and wife.

The reception was held in a large hall located in Ano Korakiana, and when we arrived there with our friends Jan and Antoinette, we were astonished to see that nearly five hundred guests had gathered to celebrate the couple's wedding.

Seated at a long table with perhaps twenty other guests, we were treated first to a *meze* that consisted of at least twenty different dishes, salads, and a main course of lamb (we saw at least thirty of them roasting on spits when we arrived), not to mention all the wine we could drink. After dinner, a toast was made to the bride and groom, and the wedding cake was cut. Then the real celebration began, which included non-stop music by a very talented Greek band with not one, but two singers that took turns singing both Greek and popular songs, a troupe of dancers and even a pyrotechnics display. I can honestly say that it was the largest and most lavish wedding reception I'd ever attended.

A few months later, a man we knew from the village passed away at the age of eighty-three, and K. and I attended our first Greek funeral. On a cold winter day we again arrived at Kontokali's tiny church only to find it packed with mourners. Once again we stood outside the chapel with a host of others from our village. The service was scheduled to take place at 4:00 o'clock in the afternoon, so the sun was beginning to set. The wind was blowing at gale force, and within minutes our hands and feet were numb from standing out in the cold. Still, we braved the elements and listened to the service over the loudspeaker system. When the service concluded, we followed the funeral procession to the village cemetery. By 6:00 that evening, the deceased was laid to rest, and we returned home to a bowl of hot soup.

Later that spring, the Kontokali village festival took place, as it does each year. Lambs are roasted on spits, booths are erected by vendors selling toys and CD's and what-have-you, and a band plays well into the night as the village people eat and drink and dance to the point of exhaustion. That year, however, it was raining on festival night – not enough to cancel the event altogether, but certainly enough to dampen spirits. The crowd was much smaller than in previous years due to the weather, but K. and I made a valiant effort to attend. At mid-night, the party seemed uncharacteristically sedate, so we decided to walk home. Passing the Kontokali church, we saw that the door was open and the lights turned up. We poked our heads inside and saw for the first time the interior of our village church. We were stunned into silence by its beauty, which only goes to show how one can miss the grandeur right in his midst if he's not paying attention. The real irony was that for two and a half years we'd lived directly across the road from the church. We'd passed by its door hundreds of times. We'd heard the bells ring out from its belfry not only for Sunday services and religious holidays, but for any number of weddings and funerals. Why had it taken us nearly five years to cross its humble threshold?

In Greece, the church is the very heart of every village. It is where weddings and funerals and festival celebrations begin and end. It may have taken K. and me nearly five years to attend our first Greek wedding, a bit longer to attend our first Greek funeral, and still longer to finally visit the interior of our village's church, but once we'd done all three, we finally felt a little less like foreigners, and a bit more like members of the community.

A LIVING ANACHRONISM

In the year 2000, K. was all of eighteen and I was forty-seven, and we came to Corfu as part of a month-long European holiday. After traveling in the Netherlands, Switzerland and Italy, Corfu was meant as a sort of holiday from our holiday, a place to unwind and rest up from the rigors of city-to-city travel. It was not only K.'s first trip to Europe, but of course her first trip to Greece. Having traveled many times in Europe, and a number of times to Corfu, I, on the other hand, functioned as an ad hoc tour guide. We stayed just outside Kontokali, but as part of our ten-day holiday on Corfu we hired a car so we might see a bit of the island.

On our first day of touring we went to Paleokastritsa for a day at the beach. We also toured the monastery and had a nice lunch in a seaside taverna. Next day, we went to Glyfada beach, where we managed to get severe sunburn. On our third day, we headed to the south of the island, a region that I had never before explored, and we were fortunate enough to discover St. George's Beach.

The shoreline at St. George stretches at least a mile, and unlike other shorelines on Corfu, waves break upon the sandy beach. The town is not crowded, only a few tourist shops and a few tavernas. *Domatias* are scattered throughout the area, but the area to this day has been spared the construction of a large hotel, so characteristic of other Corfu resorts. We spent an entire day at the beach there before returning that night well after dark.

Liking the atmosphere at St. George, we returned a second time to the area, and spent another day at the golden beach. We swam in the sea and took a long walk along the shoreline. Not wishing to make the hour-long drive back to Kontokali in the dark, we packed up our car about an hour before sunset and headed out of the town. But before reaching the crossroad that led to the north, we noticed a sign that captured our attention. It read: Visit Argyrades, an authentic Corfu village. All Welcome!

Deciding to take the villagers up on their invitation, we turned up the one-lane road as directed by the sign. The road led first through a neighborhood of modern Greek-style homes, then a bit of pastureland. About a mile along the gently ascending road we entered a dense olive grove. We followed the road a bit further, and in a matter of minutes we reached the entrance to Argyrades. There the road narrowed to such an extent that we thought it best to park the car and walk into the village.

Once inside the ancient village, we were at once glad we'd decided to make the short detour. Argyrades was obviously very, very old, a village that time had apparently left in its wake. The buildings were hand-hewn and weather-beaten; the shops were little more than cubbyholes, some without electric lights; men sat at cafés like statues carved in another century; women led donkeys laden with bundles of sticks through the cobbled streets. As we moved through the narrow alleyways, the villagers went about their business. We were surely not the first tourists they'd seen, but it was also obvious to us that not many visitors to St. George actually answered the invitation on the signpost. Dressed in modern-day clothes, we felt like visitors from the future.

Seeing a hand drawn sign that pointed the way to a church (obviously the pride of the village) we followed the path that led up a steep incline. Climbing stone steps that led to the highest point in the village, a view of not only the village itself, but of the entire southern part of Corfu, as well as the open sea, unfolded before us. At the top of the steps stood the ancient church.

From the stone paved church courtyard we watched the sunset over the glorious western coastline of Corfu. Orange shafts of watery light glinted off the waves at sea, and off the rooftops of the village's ever-so-humble homes. As dusk fell, we read the gravestones in the church's small cemetery that marked the lives of priests and parishioners alike. Both the set and the setting imparted to us an unmistakable reverence, and alone at the church at sunset, K. and I married our spirits together that evening in Argyrades.

Even as the Village of Argyrades is an anachronism in modern-day Corfu, K. and I sometimes feel as such within the world we inhabit. As odd a couple as we might appear to those around us, we seem to share the kind of love for one another so reminiscent of a bygone era – one born of and supported by fate. To us, our love and our union is as expansive as the view from the hilltop church in ancient Argyrades, and as inevitable as our presence there that evening – the evening we married one another.

We've not visited Argyrades for a few years, but the memory of that evening burns as brightly within us as the sunset we watched from the church courtyard, and our love for one another remains as vast and as timeless as that glorious vista.

SMILE! YOU'RE LIVING ON CORFU!

Whenever one moves to a new locale, especially a foreign one, he must find the basic services he will need. Those services vary according to one's preferences, but certain services are more or less essential ones and include finding a doctor and a dentist.

Shortly after I moved to Corfu I noticed what seemed to be a sharp, metallic object protruding from my gum just below one of my large molars. Since the tooth in question had had considerable dentistry in the past, I was somewhat alarmed by the discovery. Not knowing what to do, or who to call, I telephoned my former dentist in the States. After I described the situation to him, he was baffled and advised me to see a dentist here on Corfu as soon as possible. Not knowing who to see, or what to expect, I began to ask those I knew if they knew a good dentist. The English people I asked referred me to the only English dentist on the island, but with the referral came mixed reviews. One of my Canadian friends told me that she and her family went to a Greek dentist, and that they were quite satisfied with the treatment. I opted for the second choice, telephoned the surgery, and made an appointment in broken English and pidgin Greek. Besides wondering what I might find concerning modern equipment and modern techniques (not to mention cleanliness), I wondered how I was going to communicate effectively with the Greek dentist.

When I arrived at the office for my appointment, the dentist herself met me there. (Unlike in the States – and other countries, too, I presume –there was no receptionist or secretary there to greet patients). Once seated in the chair, I felt as though I'd gone back in time forty or fifty years: the place reminded me of dentist's offices in the States when I was a young child – or perhaps even before that! Still, I reasoned, dentists were performing effective dentistry long before I was born, and seeing that I was already strapped in for the flight, I had little choice but to endure the ride. Anyway, the woman seemed kind and confident, so I allowed her to have a look inside my mouth. She located the problem and conveyed to me that she could easily deal with it. One hypodermic later I was feeling no pain. In a simple procedure, she was able to remove the offending article, which proved to be a tiny fish bone; and for her service she charged me the equivalent of seventeen dollars. The service was adequate, and the price was certainly right.

In spite of the successful surgery, I was still not convinced that I'd found a dentist to serve my needs on Corfu. (After all, she hadn't even had an x-ray machine in her office, not to mention the rest of her retrograde equipment.) So the next time I needed dentistry, I decided to give the English dentist a try. Which turned out to be another debacle.

Once inside the 'surgery', I knew immediately that I'd made a big mistake. Besides being sorely behind the times in terms of equipment, I found the surgery itself to be sloppy and unkempt, and I wondered, as she examined my mouth, just what the care might be like from one who quite obviously seldom cleaned her office. One good thing did develop from the visit, however. Determining that she needed an x-ray to proceed with my treatment, and not having the proper equipment in her surgery, she sent me to an orthodontist around the corner to have a full-mouth x-ray. Entering the office of the orthodontist, I was dumbfounded by the difference, as it was at once obvious that this office was modern in every sense, as well as spotlessly clean. The x-ray was made with thoroughly modern equipment by a technician, and I was invited to have a little chat with the doctor himself.

Inside the doctor's private office, I conveyed my experiences concerning dentistry on Corfu, and Doctor Nikos only smiled as I described the disparity I'd encountered between dentistry in the States and what I'd encountered so far on Corfu. "You have the good, the bad, and the downright ugly," he told me in perfect, American-style English. As it turned out, Doctor Nikos was educated in the States, first at the University of Ohio, and later at the University of Texas. He was also married to an American woman, which was why he'd been anxious to talk with me in the first place, I suppose. Anyway, we seemed to get on well together, so I asked if he would consider performing the treatment I needed. He declined, citing that he now only worked as an orthodontist. "Then give me a recommendation," I pleaded. "Send me to *your* dentist." He smiled as he wrote the name and number on a slip of paper. Needless to say, I never brought the finished x-ray film back to the English dentist.

So meeting Doctor Nikos turned out to be a fortunate sidebar indeed! When I was finally able to see Doctor Spiros (I had to wait nearly a month for an appointment – even with Doctor Nokos' recommendation), I was truly amazed by the surgery. Not only was it immaculately clean, it was modern beyond anything I'd ever seen in America. Nowhere did I see hideous looking, archaic equipment, and surrounding the dental chair was a bank of computer screens that displayed my specific condition in great detail.

Doctor Spiros told me that he had spent nine years training in Germany, and another four years training in Switzerland. He also told me that his approach was a holistic one, that he dealt not with one problem at a time, but with the entire mouth, thereby ensuring good dental health in the future as well. I was duly impressed by everything except the cost of the treatment he recommended. Indeed, were I to proceed with his recommendations, it was going to cost me close to three thousand euros. I told him to deal with my most immediate need, and that I'd consider his recommendation for the future. He agreed as he approached with the hypodermic.

I've since visited Doctor Spiros several more times. In fact, I spent a good part of last summer in his chair as he virtually rebuilt my upper right jaw. I must say that though I am substantially poorer as a result of my weekly summertime visits to Doctor Spiros, I am completely happy with the work he has done. I can honestly say that I have never had better dental treatment, and all without pain.

As Doctor Nikos told me nearly five years ago at our first meeting, "There's the good, the bad, and the downright ugly." Thankfully, I found Doctor Spiros, thus avoiding the downright ugly. These days I have to smile at the experience of finding a good dentist here on Corfu, and thanks to Doctor Spiros that smile doesn't frighten away small children.

David A. Ross

WISHING YOU WERE HERE

I suppose it's only natural during the course of our daily routines to wish we were somewhere else. Some might say, "I wish I were anywhere but where I am," while others have a specific locale in mind. If we live in a city, we wish we were in the country; if we live in the mountains, we wish we were at the beach. My in-laws are presently in Hawaii; I wish I were there!

It's also quite common to wish for other inverse circumstances: today I have to go to work, but I wish I were on holiday; today I must cook, but I wish I were going to a five-star restaurant; today the weather is cloudy, but I wish it were a sunny day. Our longing for other, more desirable situations seems quite endless.

When I stop to think about it, all this wishing seems rather fruitless. Seldom can we immediately change our circumstance or our locale, so instead we turn to fantasy. Some might say such fantasies are healthy expressions of our innermost desires, but as we all know, they can be somewhat torturous as well. What's more, each time we engage our whimsy, we deny, if only for a moment, our present situation. It's all a matter of focus, really. All this pining seems harmless enough if not taken to extreme, but is it really so harmless?

Even as we are basically dualistic creatures, our attention, it would seem, is a singular function. In truth, if we are busy wishing we were somewhere else, we are not fully aware of the circumstances around us at any given moment, and the question begs to be answered: What are we missing while we are away?

It's hard to argue that even the most mundane moment passes without nuance. Our everyday environment, no matter where we are, is surely constructed in layers of awareness. When someone I am with points out some extraordinary feature in our midst, an element or circumstance of which I was previously unaware, I tend to feel dense as a stone, and I realize the sad limitations of my own awareness. Yet each time I become suddenly and acutely aware of my environment, I find that it is literally overflowing with sensations to which I'm normally numb. Why can't I seem to exist fully within each moment?

As a result of scientific studies of the brain, we know that each of us is equipped with a kind of filtration system. It is apparently built into us so that we are not overwhelmed by sensations to the point of hopeless confusion. The complex neuro-hormone Seratonin is responsible for regulating the amount of incoming stimuli to our brains. Even our computers (which are nothing more than a manmade representation of our dualistic perception of the universe itself) are equipped with streaming devices to ensure that the machine does not overload on too much information all at once. Even as such limitations define our perception of reality, we persist in our longing for a more complete picture; hence, we wish...

Try as we might to embrace the so-called bigger picture, we are, it seems, prisoners of our rather limited attention. And caught up in our mundane situations, fantasy is a rather alluring escape – rather like going on holiday without ever leaving home, or like suddenly being on a Corfu beach in mid-summer when in reality we are trudging through the cold winter rain on our way to work. Never mind that the rain feels invigorating as it hits our skin, or that the gray sky at that very moment casts an extraordinary light upon the building before us. In truth, fantasy will not be denied: when we desire the beach, nothing else will do, so with head lowered we walk through the rain never noticing the light of Nirvana right before our eyes.

In the end, I suppose such philosophical musing really gets us nowhere – certainly not to the beach in mid-winter. Still, on this gray Corfu morning in November, I can't help wishing I were in Hawaii – even if it meant being there with my in-laws. But alas, it's not to be, so I think I'll go outside and smell the morning dew. Small consolation, I know...

GOOGLE ME, GOOGLE YOU

Everybody uses Google. It accounts for about ninety per cent of all Internet searches. Now, Google (the company) has become involved in a number of other business ventures, including the publishing of books online and the creation of an all-inclusive world library. Some might say that Google (the company) intends to rule the Internet world, and I would not necessarily disagree with that assessment. Whatever their future intentions might be, Google is already gargantuan in scope, as is characterized by the company name which by definition means, "a one followed by one thousand zeros."

I use the Google Search Engine all the time. (I wonder how many hits Google gets each and every day; surely the number itself must be a google). I recall, for instance, one rainy day last winter when I began wondering about an old friend of mine, one I'd not seen or heard from in a number of years. My friend's name was George Delfakis. I met George in the early nineties, when I lived in Tucson, Arizona. A native of the Peloponnese, George had immigrated to Canada at the age of eighteen, and then moved to the States where he'd owned a Greek restaurant in Tucson for twenty years. I visited the Marathon Restaurant many times when I lived in Tucson, and George became my friend. At the time, I was writing my first novel, *Xenos*, and George sat with me many nights after the Marathon had closed telling me stories about his boyhood in the Peloponnese. Many of those stories eventually found their way into the book I was writing, and in fact, it was George who not only encouraged me, but also convinced me that it was possible for me to move to Greece. (On the dedication page of my novel, one will find a tribute to George). Since I hadn't heard from my old friend in several years, I decided on that rainy winter day to 'Google' him and see what turned up.

To my amazement, I found far more than I was looking for with the following Google Search: George Delfakis Marathon Tucson Arizona. What I found was both sad and troubling.

Detailed in a multi-page article, I found the account of George's death. At age fifty, George had had the body of a twenty-year-old. An avid hunter and fisherman, he ate only meat that he had killed and dressed. He was fanatic about eating only the freshest vegetables, and he swam laps in his pool every afternoon. His handshake was always firm and decisive. Yet, according to the article I read that afternoon, George had had a heart attack while chasing down a scoundrel who'd apparently executed a robbery of a young woman – right before his eyes. The article went on to give the history of the restaurant, as well as an account of his all-too-short life. After I finished reading the entire account, I closed my browser window in utter amazement. Even now, I find it hard to believe my old friend is gone, and even more amazing is the circumstance of his untimely death.

A few weeks ago I received an e-mail, one that was totally unexpected. I do not often open e-mails from unknown senders, but for some reason I did open this one. It was from one of my former students, a girl to whom I'd taught music some thirteen or fourteen years ago. The e-mail informed me that she'd located me via a Google Search. Here's what she had to say:

"I have to tell you what a large influence you have had on my life. In fact, I am who I am today because of knowing you. Your love of travel rubbed off on me and I haven't been the same since. I remember the pictures from your travels hanging on your studio walls and your exciting descriptions of the Charles Bridge in Prague. The open letters you sent from Corfu were so descriptive, and I remember your audio recordings of street performers from somewhere in Europe. My dream through my teenage years was to backpack through Europe (though it sadly never happened). When I finally went, I loved Europe as much as I knew I would, and my life is forever altered. My poor husband (who doesn't have the itch like I do) has to endure my endless rants on how amazing it will be when I take him to Italy for his first time next year. So it's your fault...I tell him to blame you...and I am eternally grateful. Julie"

Remembering Julie as a teenager, I see a girl on the cusp. She was quiet, a bit skeptical; she revealed little. Yet I do recall that she traveled quite a distance each week to attend her music lesson. As a teacher, one tries to reach each student, but one never really knows what effect he might be having. In the case of this rather private girl, I remained more or less in the dark. Now, thirteen years later (thanks to Google), we have reconnected, and I must confess that I was not only surprised to hear from one so long gone in my life, but that I was amazed and humbled to learn the effect I'd apparently had on her. You just never know...

Whether or not Google takes over the cyber-world or not, I can't help believing that their effort (and the effort of other like search engine companies) is ultimately a real bonus for users, as it not only helps us locate the information we need, but keeps us in touch where we might otherwise lose track of those no longer current in our lives. This sort of communication is not only nostalgic, it is nourishing. And what could possibly be wrong with that?

GOOGLE ME, GOOGLE YOU

Everybody uses Google. It accounts for about ninety per cent of all Internet searches. Now, Google (the company) has become involved in a number of other business ventures, including the publishing of books online and the creation of an all-inclusive world library. Some might say that Google (the company) intends to rule the Internet world, and I would not necessarily disagree with that assessment. Whatever their future intentions might be, Google is already gargantuan in scope, as is characterized by the company name which by definition means, "a one followed by one thousand zeros."

I use the Google Search Engine all the time. (I wonder how many hits Google gets each and every day; surely the number itself must be a google). I recall, for instance, one rainy day last winter when I began wondering about an old friend of mine, one I'd not seen or heard from in a number of years. My friend's name was George Delfakis. I met George in the early nineties, when I lived in Tucson, Arizona. A native of the Peloponnese, George had immigrated to Canada at the age of eighteen, and then moved to the States where he'd owned a Greek restaurant in Tucson for twenty years. I visited the Marathon Restaurant many times when I lived in Tucson, and George became my friend. At the time, I was writing my first novel, *Xenos*, and George sat with me many nights after the Marathon had closed telling me stories about his boyhood in the Peloponnese. Many of those stories eventually found their way into the book I was writing, and in fact, it was George who not only encouraged me, but also convinced me that it was possible for me to move to Greece. (On the dedication page of my novel, one will find a tribute to George). Since I hadn't heard from my old friend in several years, I decided on that rainy winter day to 'Google' him and see what turned up.

To my amazement, I found far more than I was looking for with the following Google Search: George Delfakis Marathon Tucson Arizona. What I found was both sad and troubling.

Detailed in a multi-page article, I found the account of George's death. At age fifty, George had had the body of a twenty-year-old. An avid hunter and fisherman, he ate only meat that he had killed and dressed. He was fanatic about eating only the freshest vegetables, and he swam laps in his pool every afternoon. His handshake was always firm and decisive. Yet, according to the article I read that afternoon, George had had a heart attack while chasing down a scoundrel who'd apparently executed a robbery of a young woman – right before his eyes. The article went on to give the history of the restaurant, as well as an account of his all-too-short life. After I finished reading the entire account, I closed my browser window in utter amazement. Even now, I find it hard to believe my old friend is gone, and even more amazing is the circumstance of his untimely death.

A few weeks ago I received an e-mail, one that was totally unexpected. I do not often open e-mails from unknown senders, but for some reason I did open this one. It was from one of my former students, a girl to whom I'd taught music some thirteen or fourteen years ago. The e-mail informed me that she'd located me via a Google Search. Here's what she had to say:

"I have to tell you what a large influence you have had on my life. In fact, I am who I am today because of knowing you. Your love of travel rubbed off on me and I haven't been the same since. I remember the pictures from your travels hanging on your studio walls and your exciting descriptions of the Charles Bridge in Prague. The open letters you sent from Corfu were so descriptive, and I remember your audio recordings of street performers from somewhere in Europe. My dream through my teenage years was to backpack through Europe (though it sadly never happened). When I finally went, I loved Europe as much as I knew I would, and my life is forever altered. My poor husband (who doesn't have the itch like I do) has to endure my endless rants on how amazing it will be when I take him to Italy for his first time next year. So it's your fault...I tell him to blame you...and I am eternally grateful. Julie"

Remembering Julie as a teenager, I see a girl on the cusp. She was quiet, a bit skeptical; she revealed little. Yet I do recall that she traveled quite a distance each week to attend her music lesson. As a teacher, one tries to reach each student, but one never really knows what effect he might be having. In the case of this rather private girl, I remained more or less in the dark. Now, thirteen years later (thanks to Google), we have reconnected, and I must confess that I was not only surprised to hear from one so long gone in my life, but that I was amazed and humbled to learn the effect I'd apparently had on her. You just never know...

Whether or not Google takes over the cyber-world or not, I can't help believing that their effort (and the effort of other like search engine companies) is ultimately a real bonus for users, as it not only helps us locate the information we need, but keeps us in touch where we might otherwise lose track of those no longer current in our lives. This sort of communication is not only nostalgic, it is nourishing. And what could possibly be wrong with that?

NEXUS

Each and every person is different, unique and unfathomably complex: a statement so obvious that it almost sounds trite – until one begins to think about the nature of the differences, as well as their origin. I believe that many of the qualities, beliefs and opinions that make each person who he is originate from very early messages imparted to us by our parents; and I'm also convinced that those messages congeal into a nexus point around which we fashion our lives.

Some time ago I began asking those closest to me (both friends and relatives) to answer a very pointed question: What was the predominant message you received from your parents as a child? I further explained the question, adding, "…the single message you received over and over again that seems to define the person you are as an adult." As one might imagine, the answers I receive are not only interesting, but also quite telling.

As I look back to my early years, the message I remember hearing often was, "Be an individual; don't follow the crowd!" Other ancillary messages were inevitably coupled to the primary one: "Don't believe everything you hear or read," and "Be true to yourself," and "Don't judge a book by its cover." To this day I am convinced that those early messages not only have stuck with me, but shape virtually every aspect of my life as an adult. What one sees and hears as a child truly makes a difference in the adult they eventually become.

My parents, for example, were an unlikely couple in their time. My mother was from a Russian Jewish family recently immigrated to the United States, and my father was borne to a Swedish mother and a Norwegian father, both devout Lutherans. They married just after my father returned from the war in Europe, and I've often wondered by what odd means they met, married, had children, and a lifetime together. Certainly, they were each in their own way iconoclasts, daring enough to trample upon taboos and to brave castigation from their elders and peers. Without bravado, they charted their own course, and made their own way. Until I was an adult, I had no idea just how courageous they must have been to break away so radically from the traditions in which each of them was raised.

As a result of their parentage, I too am something of an iconoclast. I've never been one to follow blindly, I've always maintained a healthy skepticism, and I continue to honor my heartfelt nature. In fact, I may have taken those often stated, early messages to the extreme: I've chosen to live apart from my native culture (and even gone so far as to choose a somewhat remote island as my home); I've not held a position working for someone else since my early twenties; I take my time judging each new acquaintance or situation; I'm passionate about my calling as an artist. Indeed, it would seem that those early messages, as well as the example my parents set, are the cornerstones of my life as an adult.

What is equally interesting are the messages they refrained from imparting. Concerning religion, I was never entreated to accept and practice the faith of either parent; instead I was told to make up my own mind, and to respect the beliefs of others. Today, I call myself neither Jew nor Christian. At best, I am agnostic, which also seems to fit my upbringing.

All in all, the examples of my 'chip off the old block' theory are both prodigious and profound. Both my parents loved art, and they made it a point to surround me during childhood with books, paintings, trips to the theatre, and so forth. They both embraced a strong work ethic, as do I today. They had friends of various nationalities and religions, as do I today. Each cultivated a sense of personal responsibility, which I also feel.

By contrast, one of my father's often-vented expressions was: "Oh my aching back!" As a result of that unfortunate message, I now spend a week each year in the shape of a question mark, my lower back in spasms of what? Outrageous acknowledgement? My mother often advised me that "The leaf never falls far from the tree," and the simple wisdom of that adage is certainly not lost to me as I hobble about cursing and complaining.

Once again, let me pose the elemental question: What was the message you heard most often as a child? Does that message ring in your ears today? Is it indeed the nexus point of your adult life? Most of those to whom I've posed this question are able to answer it easily and without pause. I suppose that is because such messages are not only obvious, but also long-lasting and very powerful ones. While it's true that we probably can't change many of our most basic tendencies, it is somehow enlightening to acknowledge their source. Personally, I'm glad for the elemental messages imparted to me as a child by my parents. They are not only strong tenets by which to live one's life, but they serve me well as an individual. (Oops, there it is again!)

David A. Ross

LADIES AND GENTLEMEN, ELVIS HAS ENTERED THE BUILDING!

Each summer on Corfu it's possible to see the 'King' perform all his (and your) old favorites one more time. From "Heartbreak Hotel" to "Suspicious Minds", from "Blue Suede Shoes" to "I Can't Help Falling in Love", my good friend Oresti Kovi, Corfu's Elvis impersonator extraordinaire, dressed to the tens and sporting a pompadour hair style and mutton-chop sideburns, croons the legendary tunes five nights a week with style and panache in packed bars and nightclubs.

Over the past couple of years, Oresti's Elvis act has become quite an event, and if imitation is the highest form of flattery, then Oresti is flattered by a number of those imitating the imitator: Elvis acts have popped up all over Corfu during the past couple of summers, though it is Oresti's lively performance that seems to fill the bars and clubs night after night. When one talks about Elvis here on Corfu, we all know whom they're really talking about: Oresti Kovi.

Even though this faux Elvis enjoys more than a little

recognition these days, it has not always been so for him. Born and raised in Albania, Oresti Kovi came to Corfu fifteen years ago. The means by which he arrived were not only unconventional, but also quite extraordinary.

One night, along with four friends, he set out to swim across the straight that separates Corfu from the Albanian mainland. From Kassiopi, one can easily see Oresti's hometown of Seranda, and on a clear day, one can even see many details, such as individual buildings, the newly constructed landing strip, or a church spire. Indeed, the distance across the straight does not appear to be long, and in fact it is only about four miles from shore to shore. As the five young, fit men in their early twenties entered the water that night, they must have thought the swim would be an easy one, and that they would soon be celebrating their arrival on Corfu. Sadly, only two of the five survived the waters that night.

Fifteen years ago, the advantages of living in Greece, as opposed to living in Albania, were more than obvious, not only to Oresti, but to many Albanians who left their homes and came to live in Greece, particularly here on Corfu. These days it is estimated that there are no fewer than five thousand native Albanians living on the island, and that figure may indeed be too low. Living here on Corfu, one is certain to make the acquaintance of any number of Albanian ex-pats. I myself know many. And while it certainly was true fifteen years ago that the disparity in quality of life on these two not-so-distant shores was, shall we say, world's apart, my friend Oresti tells me that today he's not so sure anymore that Greece offers the promise and economic advantage that he was once willing to risk his life to sample.

Oresti's history on Corfu has been both a varied and colorful one. During his first years spent on Corfu, he worked during the tourist season as a waiter. He never earned much money waiting tables, and when winter came, he searched out odd jobs to survive. Such a scenario is the rule rather than the exception for many if not most Albanian immigrants to Corfu. My friend Cosmos, for example (also Albanian and a longtime resident of Corfu), is part of a troupe of Greek dancers that performs aboard cruise ships all during the summer season, but during winter this very talented, and very spirited, young man survives by picking up painting jobs when he can. On any day in San Rocco Square in Corfu Town, one can see scores of young Albanian men gathered there to sell their labor to anyone willing to give them a day's work, and the rate at which they are paid is pathetic. Though their presence is tolerated here on Corfu, these young men are reduced to a class only slightly better than slaves, usually doing the hard physical labor that their Greek hosts and employers would rather not do themselves, or pay the going rate to a Greek workman. Besides being condemned to live as economic outcasts, Albanian immigrants on Corfu all too often suffer prejudicial stereotyping, if not outright verbal abuse. To say the least, life is not everything these immigrants had hoped it might be; on the contrary, many have grown bitter, or returned to their native country, humble though it may still be.

The winter that I first met Oresti Kovi, he had not yet begun doing his Elvis act. In truth, that winter we were both 'broke as a joke', and he and his girlfriend Teresa would come round to our apartment to visit K. and me. We shared simple meals as we schemed about how to survive until spring. It was during those visits that I learned about Oresti's deep and reverent devotion to Elvis Presley. On weekends, Oresti always sang karaoke at the Navigator's bar, but only Elvis's songs. During that same winter, Teresa sewed Oresti's first Elvis costume – by hand! For our part, K. and I helped him, via the Internet, to acquire suitable boots for his costume from a company in Texas. The boots, I remember, arrived just before his inaugural performance that spring.

Several summers have come and gone now, and Oresti

has become well established as Corfu's premier Elvis imitator. He performs at least five nights a week all during summer at several resorts across the island. Seldom is there an empty seat for his performance, and often the street outside the venue where he is playing is crowded with those waiting for a seat inside. Money is also not such a big problem for Oresti these days, as his service is in great demand during the summer tourist season. I try to catch his act at least a couple of times during summer, not so much because I'll see something I've not seen before, but to renew our friendship – one forged during tougher times for us both. I not only respect Oresti's courage and his creativity, I admire his stamina, and most of all his sincerity. We have become good friends over the years, and I deplore the way many Corfiots treat the Albanians who've come here seeking a better future for themselves and their families. Frankly, there is no excuse for it.

Unlike in years passed, Oresti does not stay on Corfu during winter, he returns to Seranda, where his mother still lives. Seldom do I have the opportunity to spend evenings with him scheming or simply sharing dinner, but all in all, his absence is for the best, I suppose. Oresti has invited me to visit him at his home in Seranda. I've never been to Albania, but I would like to visit some time. Perhaps I'll have the opportunity before long. For now, though, we catch up by phone about once each month. When we do meet up again, whether next spring or sooner, I know that our friendship will be instantly renewed, as it was one forged in hardship, and in hope. We share the knowledge that we are both immigrants here, a fact that we never forget, and even as we thank the Corfiots for having us, we deplore the manner in which they treat the Albanians, many of whom have Greek ancestry.

Next time you're on Corfu, make it a point to see Oresti's Elvis act. I don't think you'll be disappointed, because anyone who reveres the 'King' as Oresti does, and renders the songs with respect and humility and sincerity, as he certainly does, will certainly win his way into your heart, as he has mine.

Viva Las Vegas, Oresti! And long live the King!

CALL IT PROGRESS

Yesterday morning I was standing underneath an awning in Corfu Town to get out of the rain as I waited for the bus. As I waited, I became vaguely aware of a conversation between three Greek men who were also dodging the raindrops. Not speaking Greek, I did not understand much of their dialog, but what I did notice was that they were fixated on the English word, "progress". I can't be sure, but to my ear they seemed to be trying to pinpoint the exact meaning of a word, which to my understanding, has many (sometimes contradictory) definitions. I did not presume to intrude upon their conversation and offer my help as a linguist, but the topic of their talk did start me thinking.

Last summer I began noticing that throughout Corfu Town many of the old shops (those deep, dark cubbyholes stocked to the gills with linens and cookware and rugs and what-have-you) had begun to disappear, and that in their place were very modern, and very slick, boutiques – shops one might expect to find in Paris or Milan or Madrid. In fact, the more I looked, the more of these shops I noticed, and I came to the conclusion that something of a

129

commercial renaissance was underway in Corfu Town.

Being in the business of commercial promotion, I began talking to the owners of some of these new shops, and I learned that most were franchises of larger corporations based in Athens. The inescapable conclusion to which I came was that the traditional mom & pop shops that had so long been a vital part of the town's commercial landscape were indeed on their way out in favor of Greece's version of corporate dominance and redundancy. Call it progress...

What disturbed me all the more though, on listening to these men wrestle with the definition of progress, was that only a few moments before I arrived in San Rocco Square to catch the bus I had passed the longstanding site of Corfu Town's open-air market, only to discover that all the stalls had been taken down and that the entire site had been fenced off. Market no more. Call it progress?

Anyone who has visited the open-air market in Corfu Town can attest to its charm and ambiance. Peddlers sold vegetables and fruit; there was a fresh fish market, as well as a small wares market. It was a great place to stroll and watch people going about their marketing even if one was not inclined to buy something. On more than one occasion, I'd gone there myself for the sole purpose of taking photographs, and now I'm glad that I did, because it's apparently gone forever – all in the name of progress.

I began asking around about the market's sudden disappearance, and I learned that it had not been discontinued at all, rather it had been moved to a parking lot nearby the old site. Rather than assuage my sense of loss, this information made me a bit angry. There is nothing aesthetically pleasing about a parking lot, whereas the old site, in the midst of Corfu Town's everyday hustle and bustle, imparted a sense of tradition and continuity in all who visited it. I can only presume that the land where the old site existed has become too valuable for developers to ignore, so the market was displaced. I fully expect that in the not-too-distant future I shall see a row of modern boutiques where the venerable street market once served the needs of the community, and this, too, is done in the name of progress.

Only one thing is certain in this life, and that one thing is change. The practice of replacing something old with something new is universal, I suppose. Yet I can't help feeling that certain things are worthy of preservation, whatever the cost, as we tend to take our cultural identity from such institutions such as the open market in Corfu Town. After all, it was the place that mothers shopped, and their mothers before them, and so on. Traditions such as this market instill within a culture a sense of belonging, and likewise a sense of security. And while we may soon be able to buy the latest fashions from Milan instead of vine ripened tomatoes or freshly-cut parsley at the locale where Corfiots have for decades bought their produce and their fish, I can't help thinking that such a change is not progress at all, but a most disrespectful and denigrating rape of tradition itself.

What I might have told the three men who were trying to determine the meaning of this curious English word was that the word itself carries a secondary meaning as well as the primary one – a meaning which is ever-so-subtly inverse to the more dominant definition, a bit sarcastic in nature, and even a bit regretful or resigned. Anyway, that secondary meaning was the one I embraced after seeing the old marketplace disassembled and fenced off. Which, I suppose, makes me something less than progressive on the issue.

Anyway, I feel that it might, in many cases, be both prudent and wise to seriously consider this somewhat nebulous term when contemplating urban redevelopment, because what at first glance might seem like progress can sometimes lead to the destruction of not only a building (or in this case a market site) but to the loss of something far more valuable, namely the heritage of a culture.

Indeed, the ground on which the market once stood may have grown in commercial value to the point where town developers could no longer justify its use as a street market, but I must wonder whether or not anybody considered the irreplaceable loss that their decision ensured.

But, hey, that's progress!

A POOR COUNTRY

When Greece joined the European Union, it did so as the poorest country of the original members. One might have wondered why the EU was so interested in adopting such a stepchild. Certainly, Greece's economy was heavy baggage upon the backs of the union's wealthier countries. But I suppose the answer is more political than economic. After all, Greece sits on Asia's doorstep. Travel south and east from Greece and one enters the Middle East, and we all know what trouble and strife exists today in that region of the world. Or perhaps the economic ministers in Brussels knew something about the Greek economy that was not quite so obvious from the figures the country was required to submit, that being that Greece was not nearly as poor as it appeared to be.

Coming to live in Greece from the United States, the country did appear to me to be economically challenged, though admittedly my perspective came from the most surface of observations: whether or not a homeowner painted his house, or owned a clothes dryer, or kept a chicken coop behind his house. In the country I'd recently left, such things would certainly have been telling; in

Greece they seemed to be the natural landscape. I've since learned a bit more about how the Greek economy operates, and about how wealth (and the lack of it) expresses itself in this country.

My first experiences with the Greek economy came before the euro replaced the drachma as the official currency. I must say that before the Euro came into use, it was something of a challenge dealing with those ten thousand drachmae notes. I was forever doing conversions, even as I bought a pack of cigarettes or a chocolate bar. As I coped with the thousand and ten thousand drachmae banknotes, I had little idea what significance they had on a more macro-economic level. What did seem apparent was that in comparison with the States, or with other countries in Europe, life in Greece seemed to come at a reduced cost. The rent I paid, and the food I bought, were half what I was accustomed to paying in the States, and the disparity caused me to question the 'real' worth of a tomato or a loaf of bread. When the euro replaced the drachma in February of 2002, I got a big lesson in real worth, and about the true nature of the Greek economy.

One of the first things I noticed when the Greeks traded their venerable currency for the new euro notes, was that there suddenly seemed to be an unusual number of brand new automobiles on the road. Besides all the new cars, it was apparent that they were buying new refrigerators, new TV's, new clothes, and much more. I later learned that much of the money that Greeks saved was in cash, and that the reason it was never deposited in bank accounts was that it was 'black' money in the first place. Rather than declare the money by exchanging it for euros, they spent it on big-ticket items.

In a discussion with a Greek businessman, I was told that Greece is a poor country full of very wealthy people. No doubt, his bold assessment came from a lifetime's experience in Greek economics. Not long ago, I read an article in the *Kathimarini* newspaper claiming that an estimated sixty-seven percent of all transactions conducted in Greece were done so out of the scrutiny of the taxman. Whatever figures were originally submitted to the EU prior to Greece's acceptance into the economic union were surely inaccurate, and certainly portrayed the country as much less economically developed than it actually was. Of course, this misrepresentation played well to Greece's advantage, as more funds from the EU for development were allocated, needed or not.

These days I am far savvier as to how things really work, economically speaking. Truth is that one can't always judge a book by its cover. Sit in any cafe and watch as the locals pass and I guarantee you will never know who is rich and who is poor. Here wealth is simply not expressed by an ostentatious show of goods. If you really want to know one's economic status, find out how much land he owns, not how many Armani shirts he has in his clothes closet. Chances are still good, even after the euro, that a Greek has more money in his wallet than he has in his bank account. Here cash is king, and most of it is still exchanged, as the Greeks say, '*mavro*'.

There are many reasons for the origin and perpetuation of this cash-based, underground economy, the principle one being that the business community here was always, and is still, centered on 'mom & pop' style businesses (though that is slowly changing). It's still easy to barter one's services in such an economic climate, and it's easy to hide income. Certainly, the 'black' economy is not unique to Greece; it is practiced in varying degrees in every country in the world. The Greeks, however, would seem to have elevated it to an art form. I must confess that I find this ad hoc tax revolt to be audacious and somewhat noble. Of course the practice compromises social systems, even as it asserts the right of the individual to keep that which he has earned. Right or wrong, this highly evolved system of trading underneath the taxman's radar screen renders the economic statistics of the country on whole to be less than accurate, making Greece appear to be a much poorer country than it actually is. As we all know, appearances can often be deceiving, even to an entity like the EU. One must peel an onion to reveal its many layers, and just what one finds at the center of that onion might well be surprising indeed: a poor country full of very wealthy people.

LOVE IT OR HATE IT, YOU JUST HAVE TO LOVE IT

Opinions… No matter what topic might be brought up for discussion, a diversity of attitudes is bound to surface. There is a saying about the Greeks concerning this topic: "Twelve Greeks, thirteen opinions." I suspect that it is not really that different regardless of one's nationality, and whether one renders his opinion vocally or in writing, he is bound to evoke a contrary response from someone.

These days we have Internet forums to conduct dialogs. What a wonderful medium! Not only can we discuss various issues with those we meet in person, but we also have the facility to discuss virtually anything with those we've never met face to face. No matter where on the globe one may reside, and no matter what his age, or race, or religion, or physical condition, Internet forums offer a venue for discourse.

Of course, when any topic is open to a free exchange of ideas and opinions, a certain amount of controversy is bound to surface. Contributors may have a wide range of opinions on any given subject, and if a forum is lively (and if it is uncensored) those opinions are often expressed passionately, and sometimes with less civility than we might like. Be that as it may, the free and open exchange of ideas can be very stimulating, and sometimes even a bit infuriating. But I would not have it any other way, because when all is said, it is our differences – not our similarities – that make us truly interesting to one another. And from a free exchange of ideas comes new insights, and ultimately innovation.

Yet it has not always been easy (or safe) to express one's ideas openly, or to take issue with the ideas of another person or group. Poor Galileo was nearly hanged for proposing ideas that we now accept as facts. Not to mention countless others. In fact, it has occurred to me that no idea that is now widely accepted as truth ever originated from conventional thinking: each and every concept we now hold as true was once considered to be radical thinking. Still, even in this age of easy and instant communication there are those people who would wish to exercise control over not only what others think, but also which ideas and information are available to others. We have all seen the inevitable results of repression (especially concerning ideas) and most would not want to be put in the position of those who suffered through such restraints.

Granted, it is not always pleasant to have one's ideas challenged or criticized, or even belittled, but in the interest of enlightenment we must have a thick skin concerning such criticism and be willing to reveal our thoughts and ideas for the consideration of others. Without such an exchange, we reduce ourselves to the level of Troglodytes, or even dumb animals. Docile people, or societies, are easily led – usually in a direction not particularly positive for the many. Our sense of reason, our ability to discern, and the voice we have to express ourselves are nothing less than our Creator's unique gift to our species, and I personally can only wonder at those who might choose to minimize or stifle those gifts in the interest of conformity or convenience, or self-interest.

Some people love a good row; others hate it. But whether one loves it or hates it, the value of discourse is hard to deny, and I suspect that most, given the choice of free and open expression or an environment of stifling repression, would choose the former. For me, the exchange of ideas is much like the exchange of oxygen: I could not (or would not want to) live without it.

Opinions... They are our food, our mental sustenance. They make us human. So express yourself! Come on, I can take it. And so can you!

David A. Ross

WHEN EVERYTHING YOU KNOW IS WRONG

The decision to live in a foreign land is one not to be taken lightly, or frivolously. No matter how many times one has visited the country he intends to make his new home, or how much he may think he knows about how things work, there will undoubtedly be many surprises for which he cannot possibly be prepared. This much I know from experience.

Relocating to a foreign country is far more than a logistical exercise; it requires a fresh mental perspective as well. As we have all become thoroughly socialized by our native culture, it is all but inevitable that on arrival in a new land, everything we thought we knew will turn out to be wrong, or at least partially so. Usually there are no signposts pointing the way to the new protocol, so one can feel more than a little lost in his effort to adjust. Beyond the more obvious frustrations imposed by such adjustments, there is an emotional factor that will no doubt come into play, and how one deals with such challenges will certainly play a deciding role in the success or failure of the move.

Coming from America to live in Greece, I have experienced this painstakingly slow process myself, and even after more than seven years of living exclusively on Greek soil, I must confess that my adjustment is far from complete. On the contrary, I am more and more convinced that it will be a lifelong process, and one that I will never fully realize. So much of the Greek cultural life remains a mystery to me, an onion with so many layers that no matter how many I may peel away, I shall never reach its center.

No doubt, each person has his own method of coping with the many conflicting circumstances he might encounter, and whether or not he is eventually able to attain some acceptable measure of comfort is determined by any number of factors. Here are some that I have found to be important:

1) Financial viability: Many who come to live on Corfu do so having a ready-made income. At first glance this would seem to be an ideal situation, but it can also be a one-way ticket to a much less desirable circumstance: boredom. Countless times I have encountered pensioners with very little to do but sit in a pub and drink. They are there day after day, until eventually they fall off the bar stool in ruined health. I'm quite sure that this was not the so-called retirement they once envisioned – one of leisurely days in a warm climate with few cares.

To my eye, those who come here with limited funds, thereby necessitating that they work, find integration not necessarily easy, but at least possible to a degree. Becoming intimately involved with one's new culture is not only desirable but also essential, I believe. Integration helps the newcomer to feel a sense of belonging, which is an essential part of a healthy and happy emotional life. Yet, even if one is determined to work in his new culture, it hardly guarantees him a ready-made place in the working

world. Here on Corfu, one does not simply go out to look
for a job. The reality is that jobs here are scarce to begin
with, and those that are available usually go to the native
population. This circumstance demands that the expatriate
create his own niche, so to speak, and that exercise
requires that he is not only highly observant, but also very
creative. Those who come here to live that possess such
qualities are far more likely to have a successful integration
on every dynamic of life.

2) Social: Here on Corfu, making friends seems at first
to be an easy process. Not only is there a good many other
ex-pats to lend support and friendship but the Greeks
themselves are a very welcoming people. But again, there
are many layers to this so-called social integration. The
initial easy acceptance by the ex-pat community hardly
guarantees that once one has come to know his new
friends a bit more intimately, he will find their habits and
personalities to be in concert with his own. It's like
anywhere else: it takes time to get to know someone for
who he really is; and here on Corfu, one finds that many of
the stories one hears at first are but a cover for deeper, less
obvious traits.

Likewise, the much touted and revered Greek
hospitality can be a well-practiced veneer. As one
penetrates deeper and deeper into this culture, he
inevitably learns that the Greeks are like all other people.
They have their likes and dislikes, their prejudices and
misconceptions, and while their cultural bias demands that
they treat their guests with respect and dignity, and even
unbridled enthusiasm, they can be intolerant and rigid as
well.

In my experience, patience is the key to successful
integration. One absolutely must avoid making snap
decisions based on surface appearances concerning
character and circumstance. Time and endless observation
will eventually reveal at least a measure of truth, and

understanding both who and what one might be dealing with is a sure way to sidestep a multitude of social problems.

3) Personal: The reasons one might decide to live in a foreign land are certainly many and varied, but whatever one's reasons might be, he must certainly come to terms with his place in his adopted home. Just as it is impossible to take the bark out of the dog, it is also impossible to negate one's cultural roots. I am American by birth. I was raised in the American culture, and even as I might dislike, or even despise, aspects of my native culture, I am tethered to it in a way that is more or less unshakeable. And I suspect that no matter what culture one is born into, the same is true for him. In short, no matter how long I live here in Greece, or how many Greek customs or traits I might try to adopt, I will never fully escape my history, or my culture. Adapt as I might, I will always be American, and therefore a 'stranger in this strange land'. One must come to terms with his foreignness in order to live here in harmony. Even as we acknowledge what we might miss about our homeland, we must embrace wholeheartedly that which we experience in our new, chosen home. Again, to my experience, this can be an emotional roller coaster ride. Some deal with their sense of loss by returning time and time again to their homeland, while others plunge head first into the new situation. I, myself, am one of the latter, as I've not returned even once to my country since moving to Greece. Yet I certainly know others who make repeated trips to their homeland to see family and friends. I can't say I have an answer to this dilemma, but I do know that anyone that chooses to live in a foreign country will encounter it. I suppose, in the end, each person must deal with his loyalties, as well as his repulsions, in his own way.

The fact is that living in a foreign culture is no simple matter. Those who think that they will simply move to a place like Corfu and live the tourist-style life they've come to know while on holiday will no doubt end up disillusioned, and perhaps quite miserable; however, those who come here after much soul-searching, with an open mind and a patient point of view, just might find that in time they are able to fit themselves into the very narrow margin of a balanced life in a foreign culture. And if one is ultimately able to do that much, then he has done quite a lot.

WHAT WE HAVE AND WHO WE ARE

What are the most essential elements of identity? Here are a few distinctions to help us understand the answer to a most complex question:

What I have: my house; my car; my clothes; my food; my jewelry; my furniture; my computer; my books; my guitar; my money. Who I am: a body; a mind; emotions; a family member; a community member, a mortal man.

To further define our identity it might be helpful to clarify that which is not rightfully ours: family; friends, the earth.

We do not possess other people, as in my wife, my daughter, my mother, my father, my friends...

And though it may seem otherwise, we do not really own the ground on which we walk, as in my street or my land.

The person we identify as our 'self' is a matter of many non-tangible elements: character; faith; empathy; the capacity to love. The true definition of 'self' is never connected with an object. We come into the world without a material identity, and we shall each leave it in a like condition.

In our modern world the temptation to identify ourselves with material possessions is powerful and ever-present, even convincing at times; but it is wise to make the distinction between 'what we have' and 'who we are'. Only from such a position of clarity can we realize our true potential as human beings.

BAIT AND SWITCH

Lately, K and I have been entertaining the idea of moving to a different part of the island. Ever since coming to Corfu, we have lived in the village of Kontokali (a once but no longer thriving tourist village), and we've thought that it just might be time for a change. During recent trips to the north of the island, we have made many new friends in both Acharavi and Roda, and like many others, we have come to appreciate that part of Corfu. So, with a potential move in mind, this past weekend we made yet another trip to the north, this time to look at a couple of houses where we might live. Of course, we were not flying blindly on this mission, as we had already researched, with the kind help of friends, a few housing possibilities.

One of those possibilities was a recently built house just outside the village of Roda. We were already aware of the house from previous trips there, and both the accommodation itself and its location seemed to suit our needs. We made an appointment with the owner to see the house, and on Saturday afternoon we made the one-hour bus trip to the north to meet him.

The owner of the house did indeed meet us at the

appointed time and place, and after exchanging greetings we crammed ourselves into the cab of his pick-up truck for the five-minute ride to the house. Or so we thought...

Instead of driving directly to the house, the landlord decided, without consulting us, to show us a 'different' house first, one that belonged to his 'cousin'. Held captive in the cramped confines of his vehicle, we had no choice but to go along.

"This is a beautiful house with a magnificent view of the sea," he told us as we drove further and further away from Roda (our preferred location) over narrow rutted roads and through endless olive groves. After a twenty-minute drive, we arrived at the house of choice – his choice!

True to his description, the house was located on a promontory overlooking the sea, as well as the village of Sidari. Not wishing to offend, and still hoping to see the house in Roda, K. and I fell out of the cab and hiked up the long driveway to see the house, all the while knowing that we were not interested in renting it.

Putting the key into the lock, the landlord was astonished to find that he could not open the door to the house, and in fact, the lock itself came apart as he tried to turn the key. Vandals had apparently preceded us to this remote locale and jimmied the lock in their effort to enter the house. Of course the landlord was upset about the attempted break-in, and he proceeded there and then to have a twenty-minute conversation with the local police. Which was understandable, considering the situation. We waited patiently for him to finish his business.

Once the police report was made, we then climbed back inside his truck for what we presumed would be a trip to the original house we were to preview. Wrong again!

Reaching inside the glove box, the landlord produced a plastic bagful of keys, and we were off on a tour of his many properties to inspect each lock on every door. This took another hour and a half. Okay, we weren't in a position to argue, and what's more, we had no idea, after driving over endless two-track mountain roads, where we were. "What about the house in Roda?" we finally asked after each house had been inspected and determined to be secure. "I only want to rent it if the tenant will pay me for ten years' rent in advance," the landlord told us without shame.

Which brings to mind the old con game of 'Bait and Switch'. Of course the idea of paying ten years' rent in advance was ludicrous to us, and we could almost see the saliva dripping from his lips at the prospect of netting a big payday from a couple of gullible foreigners. (Yes, it has been known to happen here on Corfu). In short, we never saw the house in Roda, as it was never really for rent. Neither did we entertain the landlord's suggestion of a second meeting the next morning to see the 'house with the spectacular view' once the locksmith had come to repair the jimmied lock.

Bait and Switch – it's a game that has been played time and time again on unsuspecting and trusting foreigners by Greek property owners, but this time it was nothing more than wasted time and effort – our time and his effort. We are now re-thinking our decision to move from our familiar environment.

EAT MORE ICE CREAM

For many years I have been fascinated by what the very oldest members of society have to say about life. For me, the voice of vast experience seems to speak with a profundity gained in no other way. All too often, it seems, the oldest among us are cast aside, and the wisdom they might impart to us is ignored as we scurry about attending to the 'more important affairs' of the day. Yet, the exclusive point of view that one might acquire after eight or nine decades of experience is one that should not be ignored.

At age eighty, or ninety, or even one hundred, one's outlook may be short, but perspective is undoubtedly long. Often such people see the adventures and misadventures of life not only from a philosophical point of view, but also from a humorous one. What they have to tell us should be taken not with a grain of salt, but with respect and a bit of reverence. From no other source can we gain the unique insight they have to offer.

For example, I site the story of Jean Calmont, who several years ago, at age one hundred twenty-two, was documented to be the oldest living person in France.

Imparting a few tips for a long life to the interviewer, Ms. Calmont revealed that everyday she smoked two cigarettes and drank a glass of Port wine. When asked about her outlook for the future, she laconically stated, "Very brief, *mon ami*!"

In my early twenties, I remember reading another interview with a woman who was celebrating her hundredth birthday. When asked what she might have done differently during her life, she replied simply, "Eat more ice cream." I've never forgotten that simple metaphor, and I try to live by it everyday.

My mother was the youngest of four children, her only sister (my aunt) being the eldest. Unfortunately, my mother died at age sixty – far too young – and her two brothers followed her shortly into the hereafter. Aunt Rose, on the other hand, lived to be ninety-seven, and remained bright as a bulb until the very end. Even after I moved to Greece, I telephoned her regularly. She loved to receive my calls, and for a woman of ninety plus years, she was inexhaustible as a conversationalist. We discussed everything from family history to world affairs, books she'd recently read to a rather comic marriage proposal she'd recently received from and 'older gentleman'. Born in Europe herself, my aunt was quite thrilled about my decision to live abroad, and she told me about her visits to Italy and to Yugoslavia. Her insightful observations about my decision to move to Europe helped me to understand my own motives in a way that I might otherwise never have considered. "If only I were three years younger," she once told me, "I would come to visit you." Imagine that!

Rose also read my books with great interest and encouraged me to keep writing, no matter what. She told me that my maternal grandfather, whom I never met, had always wanted one of his children to be a writer, and she was very happy that even though none of them had accomplished the desired avocation, his wish was fulfilled in me. From Rose I learned the details of the family's immigration from Russia in the early twentieth century. Her memories of their midnight escape were as vivid as if they'd happened only yesterday, and her colorful description of the event (she was five years old at the time) fascinated me to no end. It was valuable family history that I could have learned from no one else, and today I'm very glad that I took the opportunity to learn about the events that eventually led to my very existence.

A year or two before she passed away, Rose and I had a very frank conversation about her beliefs concerning an afterlife. She told me that she did not believe in Heaven, or any other sort of life-after-death. But she was not concerned about her impending death. "If I go to sleep tonight and don't wake up," she told me, "that's okay." She went on to say, "I've had a wonderful life, and I've always tried to help people." What a legacy! What a fitting epitaph!

When Rose finally passed away a few years ago, there was, of course, great sadness among her remaining family and many friends. All who knew her recognized in her the brilliant light that shone from within. Yet even as the world is a poorer place for her passing, it is hard to feel regret for one such as my aunt, who lived not only a very long life, but one marked by a deep sense of compassion. The lessons I took from her life are ones I try to practice everyday.

So, the messages we receive from the very old are apparently clear, and apparently a bit redundant. Indulge your vices, but do so in moderation. Maintain your sense of humor, and don't take yourself too seriously. Take a risk or two. And above all, eat more ice cream.

WHO'S WHO ON CORFU?

As many of us here on Corfu are far away from our natal families, holiday celebrations are usually shared with what I like to view as our extended family – our friends and neighbors, kindred spirits all, from across the island.

This year K. and I attended several parties. Our good friend Jack, in honor of his birthday, hosted one of those events, at which English people, Greeks, Americans (including Jack's wife), and a man from Slovakia celebrated. On New Year's Eve, we attended a lavish party in Corfu Town, where we were the only non-Greeks present. We also hosted a party to celebrate my birthday.

Here on Corfu such social gatherings are always composed of diverse nationalities and backgrounds. Different languages fly about like debris in a windstorm, a sentence often beginning in one language and ending in another. Discussions are always lively and never short on interesting ideas, many of them comparing our lives here on this far-flung Mediterranean oasis. The ever-interesting mix of people and ideas always sets my analytical tendencies in motion, particularly concerning our so-called extended family here on Corfu.

For example, I recently learned that there are now more than fourteen thousand British ex-pats registered with the British Embassy. When I moved here in 2001, that number was just seven thousand. It stands to reason that if fourteen thousand are registered, then there are also many who choose not to register, making the actual number of British ex-pats living on Corfu somewhat higher. I estimate the number is actually closer to twenty thousand. Out of a total population of one hundred thirty-five thousand, that is certainly a significant number.

Of course there are other foreigners besides the British living here on Corfu. There are also a significant number of Dutch, Germans, Austrians, Italians, and Scandinavians. There are a number of South Africans, a few Canadians, Australians and New Zealanders, and even the odd American or two! More and more often I encounter new residents from Eastern Europe, people from countries including Serbia, Romania, Poland, The Czech Republic, Slovakia, and Hungary. Albanians, the most prolific non-British immigrants to Corfu, now number five thousand to seven thousand souls. My own crude estimate of non-British foreigners living on Corfu is ten thousand to twelve thousand. To say the least, Corfu is becoming a very diverse place to live. Simple arithmetic tells us that only about one hundred thousand of Corfu's one hundred thirty-five thousand residents are Greek, and many of them are not native Corfiots.

It is a well-known fact that tourism here on Corfu has been declining for the past several years (perhaps as many as fifteen years), and it is also well recognized that many foreigners are choosing to make Corfu their home. As anyone who has ever visited Greece surely knows, the Greeks, as a culture, are extremely hospitable. Still, one might wonder what they think about this influx of foreign residents. I've asked a number of Greek people about it, and almost to a person they say they embrace their new neighbors. In a world where cultural distinctions are often viewed with suspicion and even disdain, such an attitude is, if not unique, then surely uncommon. I, for one, am thankful for their open-minded perspective and for their welcoming attitude, yet Corfu is a unique place with unique concerns, and there is, as one might speculate, method in their benevolent madness.

With each foreigner who relocates to Corfu comes a bank account, be it large or small. Many new residents buy property that has long been in the hands of the native Corfiots, thereby infusing significant amounts of cash into an economy decidedly short of liquid capital. Besides buying property, these new residents patronize Greek shops and also avail themselves of the many services provided by Greek builders, plumbers, lawyers, doctors and dentists, and the like. In short, the influx of foreigners coming to Corfu to live is a needed shot of adrenalin to the local economy. Some of the foreigners bring with them skills that have been sorely missing in the Corfiot culture, and many of the Greeks here also take advantage of that know-how. There is little doubt that Corfu is waist deep in a cultural transformation – an evolution, if you will – one that seems to be taking place peacefully and amicably.

Still, as one such newcomer, I cannot help viewing the extremely rapid advancement of foreign residents as anything short of profound in its implications. If present trends continue (and all indications suggest that they will not only continue, but increase), then the character of Corfu itself shall undergo a metamorphosis at whirlwind speed. So many indications of this are already present: English as not only a secondary language, but an increasingly dominant one; the availability of not only English goods, but products from virtually every European country and beyond; the assimilation of foreign tastes and habits by the Greeks themselves! All this begs the question: Is Corfu destined to become another Gibraltar, or Barbados? My inclination is, probably yes!

Whether one views this metamorphosis as positive or

negative probably depends largely (though not wholly) on his position in the current Corfiot society. If one is British, or from other northern European countries, or even from North America or Australia or New Zealand, he finds the Corfiot culture more accommodating, and more familiar, as the months pass. If one is Greek, he may see his new neighbors as a splendid opportunity for economic profit. The mix of cultures on Corfu is anything but fragile; it has now become an accepted reality, a given, a way of life. For those foreigners who choose to penetrate the native culture, acceptance is not only tolerated, it is graciously granted. For the many Greeks now under stress from the decrease in tourism, the foreign rampage is perhaps a Saving Grace, at least economically so. (Though still far below the value of British properties, Greek real estate has increased significantly in value over the past few years, and many Greeks embrace the opportunity to sell long held land and houses to anxious foreign buyers).

What does all this mean? Only time will tell whether or not this undeniable demographic shift will continue, but I believe it will, and perhaps the trend to Anglicize Corfu will even accelerate. Many believe (including some Greeks) that the large contingent of British now living permanently on Corfu will benefit the island on whole. That remains to be seen. Myself being part of this new community of Corfiots, my attitude is biased at best and ill informed (if not wholly ignorant) at worst. Day by day we dance the dance of this cultural metamorphosis, and fate itself calls the tune. Let us all hope that the music to which we whirl remains melodic and upbeat.

GOOD DAY SUNSHINE

We're having a terrific winter here on Corfu. The sun shines most days and the temperature is consistently fifteen to sixteen degrees Celsius. Of course an occasional day of rain darkens the sky, but not like previous years when it has poured down in buckets day after day. The Greeks have a word for this sort of winter: *alkionides*, which means small summer!

It would be simplistic to say that the weather accounts for our greater sense of well being, but it certainly must play a small part. Otherwise why would so many northern Europeans look forward so fondly to holidays on sunny Corfu? But our frame of mind depends on so much more than good weather, doesn't it?

The other day K. came out of our office after a long stint working on the computer and proclaimed quite definitively, "My life is so excellent!" I did not need to reply, because I knew exactly what she meant. I feel the same way.

Not to say that we don't have our share of 'life's little tensions'. A certain amount of daily conflict goes with any territory. But I knew that she was talking about something beyond life's inevitable vicissitudes. She was talking about the so-called 'big picture.' Environment may play a part in one's sense of well-being, but it's surely only a piece of the puzzle. Also included are home, health, family, friends, work, recreation, and yes, finances. Indeed, satisfaction seems contingent on all these factors, and more!

Given one wish by that proverbial genie, some might wish for fame and fortune. Others might wish for perfect peace and security. Still others might wish away all the conflict in their lives. Not me. I'm quite content to take things as they come, one day at a time, troubles included. The most profound aspect of my good fortune is my freedom to choose my own destiny, which I take very seriously. For me, peace comes from knowing I'm in the right place at the right time, again a circumstance governed by my personal choice. With a minimum of insight (just paying attention to your inner voice), and with a sometimes bold and sometimes idiotic expenditure of courage, one can arrange the particular circumstances of his life precisely to his liking. Security, on the other hand, I know to be a lie – perhaps the greatest hoax ever perpetrated on humankind. Nor would I wish away the conflict and inherent stress in my life: without a bit of tension, our bodies could not stand erect, nor would we have much sense of purpose in our lives. As I said, I prefer to take things as they come, troubles and all, to enjoy life's gifts and to work patiently with life's little foibles. That way I too can make the assertion, "My life is so excellent!"

The sun is coming up on Corfu as I write this message, and it promises to be yet another good day on the island. Of course, from my point of view, every day is a good day. After all, it beats the alternative, at least as far as we know. I'm eternally glad that I don't know what might happen as each day dawns, and I'm equally happy to have the opportunity to participate in each day's drama. My very existence is, to me, a divine wonder, and try as I might, I can't seem to imagine a world without me in it. Each morning I wake up amazed to still be here, and grateful to whatever greater power might exist for giving me the chance to relish creation. Really, what else is there to do?

Problems and all, I will take any number of moments today to acknowledge the sunshine in my midst, and I will also try hard not to take whatever problems occur too seriously. Because I know in my heart that those little problems are my backbone, and I also know that the sunshine is my due.

My life is so excellent!

TURN-ABOUT IS FAIR PLAY

Most of those who read my column each morning are British. Some live here on Corfu, but most live in the UK and look forward to their holidays on Corfu. For many of those, it appears from their comments that Corfu represents an escape from the routines of their everyday lives. But no matter where one lives, the urge to get away and experience something out of the ordinary surfaces from time to time. That is no less true for me, living here on Corfu. In fact, during winter the need to 'get off the rock' is often at its strongest, and I must confess a pining from time to time to take a holiday in England.

I've been lucky enough to visit the UK a number of times (though not since 1997) and I must admit that it is one of my favorite destinations for a holiday. I've always found the country to be infinitely interesting, the people welcoming and ever so cordial, the accommodations excellent, and the culture on whole to be superb. Many of my English friends here on Corfu are quick to point out the negatives in their homeland, and I suppose I do likewise of my country, but visiting the UK as a tourist has always been a stellar experience for me, and I've always returned wanting to visit again in the future.

I recall quite fondly my first trip to England in 1991. Unlike most Americas who visit the UK, I did not concentrate my visit on London. In fact, I did not arrive in the UK by air, but rather by ship, at the port of Dover. My first stop in England was the village of Canterbury, and I was immediately captivated by the culture. From Canterbury I made the trip by train to Bath Spa, which I found to be nothing less than a misty dream from which I might well have wished to never wake.

Before visiting the UK I had been reading the literature of Dion Fortune, who has written any number of books on the modern-day version of the ancient Celtic religion. I was quite fascinated by her writings, and I wanted to see some of the places she talked about in her books. Of course I had also read the various renditions of the King Arthur myth, from Mallory to Marion Bradley, so the area of the southwest was of special interest to me. To fuel my fire even more, I was a big fan of Van Morrison's music, and the many references in his lyrics to those mythic sites was not lost on me. So, on a daytrip from Bath, I visited the village of Glastonbury, where my purpose was to climb to the top of Glastonbury Tor.

When I arrived on the High Street in Glastonbury on a very misty morning, I exited the bus right in front of a Red Cross resale shop. Inside the shop's display window, I saw two brass bells. I don't know quite why my eye was drawn to the bells, but they seemed to have some significance that I could not identify at the moment. Leaving the High Street, I began walking in the direction of the Tor, and I soon found a footpath leading up the hillside. Even though the weather was damp, I was in no hurry to make my way to the top, and I relished the beautiful birdsong as I climbed. Reaching a creaking iron gate, I passed from modern-day Glastonbury into the realm of ancient Avalon, and as I did, the bells from St. John's Church in the village began to chime. In perfect concert with the birdsong, the bells peeled out a symphony that I remember well to this day. All the while I climbed the Tor the bells rang out in quadraphonic splendor, and as I reached the top of the Tor, the mist rolled in from the sea to mantle the village below. Suddenly, I understood the ancient metaphor that so poetically described the Isle of Avalon. Amidst the sounds of bells and birds, I was transported through the ages, to a time when magic had real meaning.

I remained atop the Tor for about an hour, and all the while the bells continued to ring out from what seemed like every direction. Below, the village of Glastonbury was invisible beneath the fog, and in my mind the veil of ignorance and doubt was lifted to reveal the enduring substance of a great myth.

Back on the High Street, I went immediately to the Red Cross shop I'd seen on entering the village. I now understood on some less than tangible plane why the two brass bells in the window had captured my attention. I bought the bells without hesitation, and I have them to this day, a reminder of that special afternoon in Glastonbury.

Next morning, I was having breakfast at my B&B and struck up a conversation with a very proper English woman who was also staying at the house. She asked where I'd visited on the previous day, and I told her I'd been to Glastonbury Tor. Sipping her tea, she looked over the rim of her teacup and said, "Rather like walking into another dimension, don't you think?" I could not have agreed with her more.

So as I live my day-to-day life here on Corfu, I often muse not only about that day, but also about the many other wonderful experiences I've had while visiting the UK. And they are many! I'm sure I will return to England again someday, as it is a very special place in my heart of hearts. In fact, I even entertain fantasies, from time to time, about what it might be like to live there. I know many of those who do live there would surely advise against it, but still I can't help wondering what new and interesting experiences such a situation might offer. I suppose that wherever one lives, sooner or later the scenery seems a little less impressive, and the experiences fail to excite one's curiosity. It's our nature to want to experience new places, and to encounter different types of people. And perhaps it's built into our DNA to feel as though the grass is always greener just beyond our own fence.

David A. Ross

CHANGE OF SEASONS

It is that time of year when we first begin to notice the changing of the season. The intense heat of summer is finally gone, the daylight is growing shorter, the first leaves are just beginning to change color, and here on Corfu fewer and fewer tourists can be seen.

I've never been all that keen on summer – at least not since I was a child. I much prefer spring and autumn. Even winter – at least here on Corfu where it does not get terribly cold or snow – is more to my liking than summer. Summer seems to carry with it a feeling of intensity, where the other seasons are mellow – especially autumn. Living in a place that goes full tilt in summer, I appreciate the ease that autumn has to offer.

Autumn is the time of year when those of us living here on Corfu can relax a little – or at least look forward to relaxing soon. It is a time when we often reconnect with those we've not seen during the summer season because we've been too busy, or simply because it's been too hot to make much effort. Here social life moves indoors during late autumn and winter, into our homes (instead of the tavernas) for more intimate gatherings. We all seem to go into a state of suspended animation, and finally, it seems, we each have time for our more private pursuits.

This year it has occurred to me that I too am in my autumn season. I will be closer to sixty, rather than fifty years old at my next birthday, and unless I live to be one hundred twelve (which is unlikely even in Greece where longevity is quite common), I am certainly past my midpoint. Thankfully, I am strong of body and of will; I'm not planning on departing this life anytime soon. Of course, one never knows...

Just as I enjoy the turning of the seasons, I quite like this autumnal period of life. One seems to have the experience and the perspective not offered in youth, or even in younger midlife, yet one is also still quite vital, and for me at least, the feeling that the best is yet to come is pervasive.

Certainly, we all have dues to pay in this life, and mine have not been burdensome. These days, I feel truly blessed. I have my health, more or less; I am involved in a loving and nurturing relationship; I do the work I choose; I live where I want to live. Just as the leaves on the trees change color in autumn, the hair on top of my head does likewise. My shape is not what it once was, but there seems in this ever-so-subtle degradation to be certain compensations that only one approaching his *denouement* can appreciate. I have nothing to prove; time marches on whether I like it or not.

I'm not afraid of growing old, or of dying. Somehow, I sense an as yet undisclosed joy in the perspective I have yet to gain, and I'm hoping to relish that season of my life as much as I've enjoyed each of the others. For now, though, I watch the changing of the season with a sense of inevitability, and also with a sense of satisfaction; for there is certainly a force behind the ephemeral that is greater than I, and of which I am an indispensable part.

Truly, what a time this is! And I mean to relish every moment.

WHERE JOY BEGINS

Without exception, everybody wants to feel whole. Each person longs to feel secure, useful, loved. Even beyond these obvious criteria for happiness, the heart seems to call out for something more: joy.

Such a condition is not one that can be granted to us by another. It often comes over us at odd moments, quite unexpectedly, and we can neither summon it, nor can we hold onto it or conserve it as we would a sweet to enjoy later and at will. Perhaps it is not even a state that can be easily defined, though we certainly seem to know it when we feel it. To convey this overwhelming sentiment, we rely upon metaphors, such as "an unbearable lightness of being" or "joie de vivre". The feeling of pure joy, or rapture, is perhaps our only real connection point with what is truly divine.

Most of us try to arrange the elements of our lives as we might assemble the workings of a clock. We reason that if all the rudiments and principles are in place, then happiness will surely be the result of our effort. Yet a well-ordered life yields little more than complacency, and it often carries with it a sense of longing that is not always easy to identify specifically. This yearning, I believe, comes straight from the heart, or soul, and is a not-so-silent message to us that rapture is our rightful condition as human beings. It does not seem to matter how often we are told to be satisfied with our lot, or to be thankful for what we have, the heart, or the soul, seems to want what it wants: bliss, wonder, pure joy! Still, the question remains: How does one enter (let alone sustain) this rightful realm of exultation?

The older I become, the more I seem to experience this illusive yet so very desirable state of unconditional happiness. The temptation to try to explain or 'quantize' this unexpected yet pervasive feeling is hard to resist, but I seem to have learned over the years to allow a space in my heart and mind for the unexplainable, particularly when it feels so divine; and in giving up the need for definition, or control, I seem to cultivate that which is desirable all the more. I have become convinced that the cultivation of real joy in one's life revolves around the time tested idea of following one's heart, but even as we all acknowledge the wisdom of this simple adage, we often resist it as well. Why?

The answer is that following one's heart doesn't always make rational sense. In fact, it often flies in the face of the god we call logic. Were I to have bowed to that god, I would not be married to the wonderful woman with whom I now share my life, nor would I live on this beautiful island a world away from where I was born and raised, nor would I be pursuing the career I find so very satisfying. It would seem that following one's heart should not be such a difficult pursuit, and in fact should be the most natural course of all, yet because of all the messages we receive each and every day, messages that contend for acknowledgment as unequivocal truth, messages that tell us that trials and suffering and sacrifice and pain are unavoidable, we balk at the notion of our rightful bliss.

When all is said and done, it takes both vision and

courage to do as Joseph Campbell, the writer and philosopher, entreated us to do: to "follow our bliss." And one without the other will not do. First, we must identify that for which our heart yearns; secondly, we must act upon that vision. Easy to say; but not so easy to do. Yet, if a circular state of yearning is the inevitable result of not doing so, and if unadulterated joy is the reward for our vision and our courage, then where is the debate that so often rages beneath the surface of our everyday analysis? Why are we so reticent to acknowledge our divinity? We must each, in time, cease to resist our God-given potential and allow ourselves to become the person that our heart of hearts envisions. In so doing, we experience ourselves as our Creator made us – O so very joyous!

THE MORE THINGS CHANGE, THE MORE THEY STAY THE SAME

It is sometimes said that the more things change, the more they stay the same. This is, of course, an oxymoron, yet we often find a bit of truth in such nonsensical statements. I find that that is true when talking about Greece, and Corfu in particular.

In many ways, Corfu is a study in contractions. For example, summer is hot and dry and it almost never rains; winter is chilly and the rain is so frequent that one might begin to think he's living inside an aquarium. Corfu Town is busy and quite cosmopolitan; the mountain villages often seem bucolic if not downright backward. My neighbor, a lifelong Corfiot woman in her seventies, still grazes her goats in the open field opposite my modern apartment; her son books clients for his tour boat via the Internet. So it's true: the more things change, the more they stay the same.

I came to Greece for the first time in 1989, and I was struck by the elemental way in which most people then lived. Back then, eggs still came from chickens, not from a cardboard container bought at the supermarket. In fact, there were no proper supermarkets, only small grocery shops where people seldom paid in cash. Instead, a ledger was kept by the shop owner, and if money was not available when it came time to pay, settlement was often taken in trade. It was not hard to believe that Greece had been forgotten by time. Until I boarded the ferryboat to Athens and saw a group of Greek children plying a video game on board the ship. At that moment I understood that Pac Man was spelling out the end of an era.

These days, one must look a bit harder to find remnants of the old way of life on Corfu. In Corfu Town, one can stroll the narrow alleyways of the Venetian quarter and still see city people living as they did decades ago, but just around the corner one is likely to see a modern boutique full of expensive fashions from Italy or France. Take a drive through any of the venerable mountain villages and you will undoubtedly see old men sitting at the local café smoking roll-ups, drinking ouzo, and playing a game of Backgammon, but these days they hardly seem to notice as a tour bus passes, grinding its gears and spewing diesel exhaust in their faces.

In Greece, as in other European cultures, tradition is a way of life. Often the celebrations practiced today are the same ones practiced by one's great grandfather. Such traditions are the cornerstone of a society, yet in many cultures the demands of the modern world leave less and less time to properly observe or commemorate the customs of old. Even as something is gained with the coming of so-called modern conveniences, no doubt something is lost as well – perhaps something very important. Yet I wonder whether such important traditions are really lost, or whether they are simply observed in new and different ways. I suppose time will eventually answer that question, because even in Greece time is the inevitable constant.

Generations may come and they may go, but look

closely at the face of a man or woman passing in the street and you're likely to be looking at an image of one long gone. Seen from that perspective, I guess it's true: the more things change, the more they stay the same.

ABOUT THE AUTHOR

David A. Ross was born January 6, 1953 in Chicago, Illinois. He attended William Rainy Harper College for three semesters before dropping out. After being excused from military service on a physical deferment, he moved to a remote area of northern Idaho, where he lived a subsistence lifestyle in a rustic log cabin without plumbing or electricity for more than a year. Returning to Chicago, he worked for Follett Publishers for a short time before relocating to Denver, Colorado. There he taught music for twenty-five years, wrote three unpublished novels, and worked as an associate editor for *Southwest Art Magazine* before moving first to Arizona then to New Mexico.

From 1987 through 2000, he engaged in a series of twelve extended trips to Europe, as well as several to the South Pacific. In 2001, he relocated permanently to Greece where he currently lives with his wife, author Kelly Huddleston, and works as an author, editor and Internet developer. *The Virtual Life of Fizzy Oceans* is his sixth published novel. Also to his credit is *Sacrifice and the Sweet Life*, a collection of short stories and poetry, and *Good Morning Corfu: Living Abroad Against All Odds*, a memoir.

Made in United States
North Haven, CT
27 June 2023

38297129R00098